A magnificent evocation of era and a vivid portrait gal eminent and the eccentric, Si well's five-volume autobiography, LEFT HAND, RIGHT HAND, is regarded as one of the richest and most versatile literary accomplishments of our time.

A succulent postscript to this great saga which the London *Sunday Times* has called "one of the wonder-works of the twentieth century," TALES MY FATHER TAUGHT ME tells more of Sir Osbert's adventures with his preposterous and endearing father. We renew our acquaintance with the irrepressible butler, Henry Moat, Sir George Sitwell's "foil on so many trips in search of the wildest geese," carrying out, so far as was possible in an imperfect world, Sir George's instructions. We meet numerous unconventional relations and come face to face with some of Sir George's "friends"; we wander once again through the gardens at Renishaw, meticulously laid out according to Sir George's highly original plan; we share Osbert's wonder at his father's pronouncements as collector, host, traveler.

We see Sir George himself — striding through his estates, carrying a spyglass so as to be able to "obtain the distant with limitless expense in the early 1900's.

# TALES MY
# FATHER TAUGHT ME

## BY SIR OSBERT SITWELL

LEFT HAND, RIGHT HAND!

THE SCARLET TREE

GREAT MORNING!

LAUGHTER IN THE NEXT ROOM

ENGLAND RECLAIMED AND OTHER POEMS

NOBLE ESSENCES

TALES MY FATHER TAUGHT ME

The Author at Home

# TALES MY

# FATHER TAUGHT ME

### An Evocation of Extravagant Episodes

Sir Osbert Sitwell

WITH ILLUSTRATIONS

*An Atlantic Monthly Press Book*

LITTLE, BROWN AND COMPANY
*Boston*                    *Toronto*

# ACKNOWLEDGMENTS

My acknowledgments are due to the Dropmore Press and to Messrs Gerald Duckworth & Co. Ltd, under whose auspices 'Hortus Conclusus' appeared as a preface to my father's book *On the Making of Gardens*; to the Editor of *Lilliput* in whose magazine 'Making a Bolt for It' first appeared (to Messrs Macmillan & Co. Ltd, under whose auspices it appeared in my book *The Four Continents*); to Mr John Lehmann, who first published, in the *London Magazine*, 'Recollections of An Awkward Afternoon in Knightsbridge', and to the Editor of *The Reporter*, where 'Unusual Holidays' appeared under the title 'My Father's Excursions and Alarms'.

I thank Mr Thomas Mark for his help with the proofs and Miss Andrade for her work on them.

I wish to thank the *Atlantic Monthly* for permission to reprint the following chapters: Chapter 9 'The Adventure of the Phantom Tax-inspector', Chapter 14 'Unforgotten Feasts', Chapter 18 'Creating', Chapter 19 'A Rap Over the Knuckles', Chapter 24 'Magic', and Chapter 28 'The New Jerusalem'.

I also wish to thank *Vogue* for permission to reprint the following chapters: Chapter 12 'Ideas from the Bureau', Chapter 15 'By Rail and Boat', and Chapter 20 'Popularity'.

# CONTENTS

## CONTENTS

The author wishes to thank Hans Wild for the photographs in this book. The credit due him was inadvertently omitted.

# ILLUSTRATIONS

# INTRODUCTION

THE chief object of a preface or introduction is to give an author the chance of tilting his book at the correct angle for the reader, and sometimes to explain how it came to be of a certain form and why it developed as it did. Thus, the origin of this book is comparable to that of jewels. When a large gem has been detached from its matrix to be cut and polished there inevitably remain fragments of precious stone. To these the expert artificer then turns his attention, proceeding to fashion them, however small they may be, into separate ornaments, or parts of them. Similarly, after the life-size portraits of my father and myself emerged from the five volumes of my autobiography, *Left Hand, Right Hand!* many memories of him that I had been compelled to omit, for reasons of the general design and by the laws immanent in every individual structure, seemed to claim my attention with a vivacity of their own. This book came into being in this way, and has been written with no other object than to engage the interest of the reader: but I hope that because I have, after this fashion, declared my purpose, he will not accuse me of levity or assume that I do not realize the tragic implications under the smiling lawns, or perceive the flames and fury of great catastrophes veiled behind flimsy screens. Nor should it be taken for granted that it was easy to write. It was not. Indeed, I experienced the same feelings as must have afflicted Sir Arthur Conan Doyle when confronted with the composition of *The Return of Sherlock Holmes*.

My father had become more finely drawn with the years, and the gothic age in which he had for so long chosen to immure himself had left its mark on his appearance, so that from the elegant young man of the eighties, who was depicted by Frank Miles and by Du Maurier in pencil drawings, he had come to resemble a bearded medieval effigy stridden down from a tomb. His energy, however, even when he was resting in bed, remained undiminished, and he still threw himself—and any other person he could find within range—into every activity in which he was interested. The only other sign of age that he showed as he grew older was that he appeared at times to suffer from what Bernard Shaw, inventing a name for it, and thus isolating and focussing a widely prevalent condition, called a *time lag*. For instance, when my elder nephew was two years old my father looked down one day at the innocent infant lying peacefully asleep in his perambulator and remarked to me in a sentimental voice:

'I do hope that they won't forget to teach the little man to sing after dinner. Nothing makes a man so popular.'

When I made an effort to explain to him that if today a man tried to sing after dinner he would be more likely to be lynched than applauded, he became annoyed and reiterated:

'Nonsense! Nothing makes a man so popular!'

Another figure must be mentioned who comes back into these pages. The reader of *Left Hand, Right Hand!* will recall Henry Moat, now family butler and formerly my father's foil on so many trips in search of the wildest geese. His return to the household after several years was the most welcome event.

## INTRODUCTION

It only remains for me to explain that the papers which follow are treated singly. I do not attempt to arrange them in strict chronological sequence: albeit they have their own inherent order, so that each episode is essential to the book of which it forms a chapter. I trust that in perusing it the reader will become further acquainted with the ways of an exceptional man and an exceptional parent, and that when he speaks in these pages the reader may catch momentarily the very run and intonation of his voice. . . . Now let us embark for the Sweet South in the early nineteen-hundreds.

# HORTUS CONCLUSUS

## MY FATHER AND THE GARDEN

I N T H E happy days of the far-off first decade of the nineteen-
hundreds, about the time that Princess Ena became engaged
to King Alfonso, that Melba was singing in *Madame Butterfly*,
that Miss Lily Elsie was appearing in *The Merry Widow*, in
short, in the golden days of good King Edward, a visitor in
the spring or autumn to any of the great Italian or remarkable
Sicilian gardens, especially those that were more remote,
might have chanced to see a tall, distinguished-looking
Englishman with a high-bridged nose, and with fair, fine hair
and a slightly darker golden moustache, flourished upwards a
little in the manner of Kaiser Wilhelm's, seated on a bench,
regarding his surroundings with analytic concentration. He
would be wearing a grey suit and a wide-brimmed hat, a
striped linen shirt with a stiff white winged collar, and starched
cuffs fastened by large carbuncle links; probably he would be
sitting on a circular rubber air-cushion shaped like a lifebuoy,
so well known a seat-mark in the daily life of the Reading

Room of the British Museum, while slung round his body as if he were at a race meeting would be a leather case containing a pair of binoculars, and beside him—for he took care to sit in the shade—a sun-umbrella lined with green. Not far off, within the carrying of a voice, from the thick blackness of an ilex grove would peer a ponderous figure, watchful, but with an eye for those who passed as well as for the safety of the rectangular, varnished wicker box in his custody, which each day contained a cold chicken. Over one arm would be folded a thick coat. . . . As he stood there he had something of an air of a night watch on a ship, and his appearance, though his skin was bronzed, or indeed copper-coloured, was as northern and national as that of the gentleman on the bench. He, meanwhile, had taken an envelope out of his pocket and was scratching on it with the stub-end of a pencil remarks angry or meditative; crossly, how a gardener had removed the patina or the lichen from a stone moulding since last he was here, or, reflectively, comparing the merits, where an effect of mystery was desired, of broad shaded ilex with thin-spired cypress, or of the different hues, textures, and sounds of varying kinds and speeds of falling water, and the sense of coolness and peace thereby induced. . . .

The visitors might perhaps enquire—as often they did when they got back to the hotel—who the English gentleman might be, and who the nautical figure hovering so heavily in the background—and the answer would come, Sir George Reresby Sitwell and his servant, Henry Moat. For in those years my father was busy collecting material for the book he planned on gardens.

In 1900 he had suffered a bad nervous breakdown and had decided in consequence to give up politics. In the ensuing years he travelled much in Italy, and of his recovery there the book was the fruit. He had already written several works of an historical nature, or illustrative of the manners of some

[16]

particular period, but had issued them from his own printing-press. They had not been for sale. But this new volume was to be published by Murray's and its aim was high, for I recollect his saying to me that he hoped it would rank in the future with Bacon's essay, *Of Gardens.*

*On the Making of Gardens,* as it is called, certainly stands as the most complete expression in my father's writings of one facet of his personality, of one concentration of his interests—but there were hundreds of others. Though he worked so hard at all the innumerable matters on which he was engaged, the truth is that he found it difficult to finish anything. The garden at Renishaw remains—and is now likely to remain—uncompleted in its detail. And the family-history, at which he had worked for two decades, was found after his death with still one chapter lacking.

Time seems to have been too short for him in his span of eighty-three years, and only this one book is an idea of his conceived, attempted, and completely achieved—whatever may be judged of the achievement—wholly realized down to the last comma and the final full-stop. Moreover, when setting himself to anything he spared no pain, either to himself or to others—it would often have been, in result, better if he had. Thus, before beginning to write the book, he spent endless hours mastering the full intricacies of English grammar, under the tuition of Major Viburne, who appears as a fitful—in every sense—shadow in the pages of my autobiography, and who knew much less about syntactic matters than did his pupil. In brief, my father took too much trouble. In order to write a sentence on the psychology of garden-making he would read a hundred slightly obsolete technical volumes, nor would he always afford his imagination sufficient room for its full sweep, since he relied overmuch on notes. (One difference between the journalist and the writer resides in this, that the first makes jottings and directly transcribes from them, while the second allows—or should allow—the subject matter of his book to grow organically, like a plant, in the mind and on the paper.) Thus, in illustration of what I mean, I once saw my father setting off from the door at Renishaw in a very old carriage, about eleven on a September night. As usually he went to bed at ten, I was surprised, and enquired what he was doing. 'Just driving down to Eckington Church to observe the effect of moonlight on the tower,' he replied with a flutter of his hand, as if conferring a favour upon the edifice; 'I want it for my chapter "Eckington Church in the Thirteenth Century" in *Tales of My Native Village.*'

Howbeit, never was any book more pondered upon at every stage than were his garden essays. For hours the author would lie on his bed wrestling with each current problem, and if Henry's footstep was heard in the passage, or a hotel housemaid dared to wipe and rattle surreptitiously the door handle—a favourite trick when a writer is at work—he would dart out of bed, clearing his mosquito net as if by magic, open the door with a snap, and look out blandly, while making at the same time a humming noise which held in it—if you listened carefully—an icy-cold but terrible menace. (Strangers, however, were apt to mistake this sound for one engendered by happiness, and in consequence often received surprises.)

Unfortunately, then, as I have said, his energies were dissipated over a field too broad for their employment. But though he was adept at taking hold of the wrong end of a thousand sticks, yet when by chance he seized the right end his grasp of it was remarkable, because of the intellectual power and application, as well as the learning, which he brought to his task. And in the book I have mentioned, *On the Making of Gardens*, we have a complete work containing a great deal of thought and couched in phrases often of stilted beauty, and even if the whole volume from its opening 'Time is a wayward traveller' down to the closing sentence which begins 'Flying shafts of silvery splendour . . .' carries for us the haunting and mocking echo of Sir Austin Feverel's *The Pilgrim's Scrip*, even if fountains are throughout inclined to 'plash', and the 'goat-herd' to figure overmuch in a landscape not untouched by Alma-Tadema, still, it is none the worse for that, being a genuine period-piece, instilled with considerable imagination, influenced by the philosophies current ten years earlier, and with, not far behind each page, those crepuscular sensations made fashionable by Maeterlinck, together with a reverbera-tion of the august, if far-fetched, rotundities of Walter Pater. Moreover—and this is where he took the *right* end of the stick—the principles he enunciated (so my gardening friends, whose judgment I trust, have told me) are invaluable in the practical design of gardens, in the counterpoint of light and shade, and the correct employment of water as a device for variation.

In short, he knew what he was talking about, having observed, noted, and practised. His knowledge of gardens—Italian, in particular—was unrivalled (several later writers have had recourse to the lists obtained from him), but not, I hasten to add, of flowers, about which, paradoxically to English ideas of the present day, no man knew or cared less, for he had early imbibed the Mediterranean conception, imposed by brightness of climate, that a garden is a place of rest and peace, and in no way intended for a display of blossoms (for that, you had 'a flower garden' away from the house, and hidden). Such flowers as might be permitted, had, like all else in good taste, to be unobtrusive, not to call attention to themselves by hue or scent, but to form vague pointillist clouds of misty colour that could never detract from the view, and to infuse into the

air a general sweetness never to be identified. The pastel-shade
sweet peas and stocks of the nineteen-hundreds, love-in-the-
mist, a few washed-out roses, and a kind of reed with a blue
flower—these passed muster: but even they were sacrifices to
my mother's insistent though contrary demands for scent and
colour. 'Horticulturists' blossoms' were what he most detested,
and, to make a personal confession, I remember that as a
schoolboy on holiday, when my father had been particularly
disagreeable, I used always to go into the garden to tend a
rhododendron that carried a purple blossom of a peculiarly
obtrusive and fiery appearance which he could see from his
study window, and which greatly offended his eye, although
for some reason or other he never eradicated the shrub in
question. This I did because I had been told by someone that
if you removed the dead racemes from a branch it would
flower again, only more flagrantly, the following spring.

To return to his book on gardens, I remember well the
initial stages of its first publication, for I had never before seen
galley proofs, and my father gave them to me—I was sixteen—
to read, with his corrections marked on them (I little knew,
then, how such flat paper serpents were to entangle and devour
my life, as if I were Laocoön). And I used to take them into a
corner of the small apartment which we had rented that year
in Florence, to revel in the sense of importance which this new
acquaintance with the technical ways of the literary world
conferred upon me. . . . Not only were these the first corrected
proofs I had seen, they were, alas, also the first I ever lost! . . .
Eventually, after a week of utter ignominy and disgrace, they
were found in a cupboard in my room where, of course, I had
placed them for safe keeping. Later in the year—for publishing
was then a quicker business altogether—my father's great
moment arrived, and the book came out—I think in August

1909. But, it is sad to recall, little more happened. One or two appreciative essays such as were written in those more leisurely days appeared in the weekly papers. He, and I, waited . . . but the rest was silence. Naturally he was disappointed, and blame was distributed impartially, some of it no doubt coming to me, but a good deal being placed to my mother's account.

I remember, too, his remarking of the top cover of his book, which was concealed under an azure dust-jacket, but displayed in bright colours the hardest and most stilted of garden vistas, that 'Murray's have managed to contradict by the design on the outside of the book every rule I have formulated inside it.' . . . However, he was pleased with the printing, if not with the reception. And I think that the actual moment of the appearance of the book was most pleasant for him. He had been ill, as the reader knows, and the process of study in gardens had healed him. The publishing of his work had constituted, moreover, a declaration of independence, and an affirmation of faith. It must have brought back to him lovely sunny days spent in his own company, which he always greatly enjoyed, with Henry and the luncheon-basket discreetly within call. Sometimes he took me with him, and on these occasions he was at his most amiable. There were, as well, adventures, such as that of which I heard subsequently from Henry, though I was not myself present. My father was meditating, just before the hour when the garden was to be closed, at the very bottom of the terraced slopes of the Villa d'Este, between the giant cypresses. He was deep in thought when four ancient *custodi* advanced on him from the four different quarters of the compass. Immediately concluding that the old men were brigands (for he always lived at least a hundred years before his time), he, as Henry put it, 'fair biffed 'em with his umbrella. You could hear 'em squawk half a mile away! But Sir George

[21]

was as cool as a cucumber and called me, saying: "Henry, the weather has changed. I had better put on my coat." ' . . . From such escapades, he, alone of living men, seemed qualified always to emerge victorious and scot-free. It was enough in those days for Henry to explain that his master was an English *signore*.

The effect, however, on my father of the lack of success of his book was considerable. He had, he told me, hoped to earn by it, now that his world was threatened by Lloyd George's Budget, something to leave to my brother Sacheverell. This hope was disappointed. And then there was another side to it. Many of my mother's friends, violently opposed to books in general, now regarded him as a traitor who had placed himself on the wrong side of the fence. Only the Bevy, which I have described elsewhere, sent up at his approach somewhat mildewed hosannahs of faint artistic praise. Meanwhile, he set himself to problems that were more immediate and practical than the theories of garden design. He arranged to send me to an army-crammer's, from which I was seldom allowed to escape—and when I did make a sortie and go home was rarely greeted with rapture. Then he had long been at work on an invention—a stick which would discharge vitriol at mad dogs and thus dispose of them. (There had been an epidemic of hydrophobia in England some twenty years before, but he had never as yet completed or patented his idea.) To this matter he now gave his mind. In addition, he made more miscellaneous notes: *Rotherham under Cromwell, Sheffield in the Wars of the Roses, Court Formalities at Constantinople, Marriage Chests of the Middle Ages, How to Preserve Fruit, The Correct Use of Seaweed as an Article of Diet, Sacheverell Pedigrees, My Views on Democracy*; each of these, and of a thousand other subjects, had a box devoted to it. These boxes were specially made for him, to contain half-pages of foolscap, and were fashioned of a material the colour of an aubergine, and in texture like a skin with goose-flesh. . . . Indeed, in everything connected with writing he had his own ways. His pens were of a fine, scratchy variety, composed of three long nibs and holders, each made entirely of one piece of metal. Three of these fitted together made a small metal rod which he could carry in his pocket without danger, but they were so thin as to render his handwriting even lighter and more spidery than it would have been in any case. For the rest, if he could not write about gardens with success, at least he could make them in the world of actuality. He abolished small hills, created lakes, and particularly liked now to alter the levels at which full-grown trees were standing. Two old yew trees in front of the dining-room windows at Renishaw were regularly heightened and lowered; a process which I then believed could have been shown to chart, like a thermometer, the temperature of his mood, and to which he always referred as 'pulling and dragging'. ('That oak tree needs to be pulled and dragged!') From the wooden towers constructed for the purpose in the lake and on the hill he would measure and survey. His head throbbed with ideas, the majority of them never to be put into practice. Glass fountains, aqueducts in rubble, gigantic figures, cascades through the woods, stone boats and dragons in the water of lake and pool, blue-stencilled white cows 'to give distinction to the landscape', many of these schemes, alas, remained where they were born. But they were a fine exercise for him, and a diversion. And it must be remembered that he would be occupied, too, every day in instructing all those about him in whatever was their speciality, while at the same time he was, besides, ferociously engaged in combat over his own affairs; for, as he rather piteously remarked to me, 'One has to think of *oneself a little*.'

[23]

2

## ALL ON A SUMMER'S AFTERNOON

A NY attempt to halt the flight of time and to hover for a
moment above selected incidents is always far from
easy for a writer—especially when the method of dating
prevalent in the family circle and household is a private system;
as in my home where everything was dated by my father's
beard. That was the Great Divide. 'It happened the year after
Sir George grew his beard,' the gardener would say, or my
mother would remark: 'That was not long before your father
grew his beard.' The afternoon of which I am writing, however, is easy to place. It was in the year 1909 (before my father
grew his beard) when I was sixteen—one of many awkward
ages—that my mother administered to my father a severe
esthetic shock.

It occurred at the beginning of the summer holiday, and
my father had not paid a visit to Renishaw for nearly twelve
months. He had been travelling in Italy and it was in the
autumn of the same year that he was to buy Montegufoni.

[24]

Now, however, the family was gathered together again at Renishaw, and I remember most vividly this particular day there, because, among its other memorable features, it was on the same afternoon that I experimented first with tobacco—or rather that tobacco first experimented with me, for it was a one-sided tussle. I had appropriated from my father's study one of the very strong Egyptian cigarettes that he then smoked, and took it to the end of the garden, where there were some chairs put out. I sat down and lighted it. I had for a long while noticed the delicious aromatic fragrance of these cigarettes, and how blue was their smoke, as it lay on the air in layers in my father's study. So now I inhaled deeply once or twice—and within a few minutes felt ill beyond the reach of human aid. I am convinced that not even the first pipe of opium can have more effect on a neophyte than does the first cigarette of a lifetime. Why on this single occasion should a cigarette produce such consequences and never again? Though some factor must be present to account for the deadly malaise that ensues, I have never heard an explanation given that was satisfactory. Be that as it may, there I was immobilized, in a chair at the end of the garden in a trance-like condition for an hour or more; a state rendered not less alarming by the fear, indeed almost the certainty, that my father would come out, find me, and ask me to accompany him on a tour of the garden. It would be impossible for me to refuse, though I could, for that period, only have accomplished it by crawling on all-fours, an innovation I could not imagine would win his favour or even approval. Fortunately, however, he did not appear for a long time—perhaps the Sacheverell pedigree was giving him trouble—and I was able to walk about again by then and had decently interred the cigarette which I had been obliged to throw down on the ground in a hurry.

[25]

My mother, contrary to habit, was the first to appear—but she, too, had suffered a shock. . . . In those days of courtesy to employers it was unusual for them to hear anything but good of themselves, nor were they accustomed as yet to Lady Chatterley's language, or to be addressed except politely and formally—none of that free and easy manner that pertains today to the new equality; no such greetings as: ' 'Morning, chum! I'm taking a day off today.' No, things were different. . . . My mother, then, was walking down the long stone corridor to speak to the housekeeper, when she saw a very small child strapped into a perambulator just outside the door of the Housekeeper's Room. My mother, who was devoted to children, stopped for a moment to speak to the infant, though she was too young, my mother thought, to talk much. Imagine her astonishment and consternation when the little girl—for such she was—wagged a fat, warning finger at her and pronounced, with a diction so exquisite that it would have done credit to a great actress, and without a trace of the local rough northern dialect, the unexpected words:

'You jigger off, m'lady.'

The child's mother, a former housemaid who had married a miner, heard the words of her offspring and rushed out and apologized, adding: 'I'm sure I don't know where she picks up such expressions. Certainly not at home. Her father is always on to her about it. He says she swears worse than any man in the pit.'

This my mother was relating to me in the garden when my father arrived on the scene, in his usual summer rig, with his binoculars slung round him, ready for the distant views. For a moment he surveyed the prospect and for the first time suddenly perceived a construction of, apparently, lattice and flimsy twigs, with some very ostentatious roses trailing about on it.

It only escaped being a pergola by its plainly very temporary nature, just as the rambler roses on it only just escaped being Dorothy Perkins. That was the most that could be said for it. It—the near-pergola—stood in a conspicuous position, technically beyond the confines of the garden but in the direct line of view. As the full enormity of this skimpy ornament dawned on him, my father gave what is so seldom encountered in real life, though it abounds in mid-Victorian novels, 'a hollow groan'. His rules for the formal garden were, as I have explained, that nothing in it should look temporary and, further, that the flowers should be kept in their place and not permitted to challenge with high colour the prospect of lake and hill and woodland. No flowers should in fact be brighter than a love-in-the-mist, its pale blue petals obscured by green veils; that was the most gaudy blossom allowed.... Therefore, at first, he could hardly believe his eyes.

'Ida, what on earth is that extraordinary thing over there?' he called to my mother, pointing at the object.

'I like colour in the garden, George,' she replied, 'and I can see it from my bedroom windows, so I told Betts to have the roses planted there as a surprise for you....'

'It certainly has been a surprise! It must be taken down at once. It ruins the whole effect of the garden and, besides, it's just where the wooden tower is to be put up so that I shall be able to see clearly the distant views from the level of the proposed new terrace.'

Not much could be seen from my mother's bedroom windows, since she had obscured the view with high window-boxes, which were planted with different kinds of sweet geranium. The more these flourished, the less you could see. My father, however, did not so much object to them because their desultory flowers were sparse and noncommittal in hue.

Now my mother's dog began to chase busily a non-existent rabbit through such flower-beds as were allowed, leaving behind him on the air a series of excited little barks and on the ground a trail of broken flower heads, the result of his impetuosity—the dog only noticed a rabbit when there was not one there. My father watched him patiently. He commented:

'I must say *I* don't see anything for him to chase—but probably there is,' and with a note of despair in his voice he added: 'Ernest Betts and Hollingworth between them have let the rabbits into the garden and goodness knows when they will be got out!'

Indeed, they were quite tame and at certain hours could be seen playing some game they had apparently invented, running and jumping in and out of the croquet hoops. In the early morning and late in the evening was the time to see them, and if you looked out of window from an upper storey then, you could discern them turned to gold by the lateral rays of the sun; though among them was a black rabbit, usually, I thought, the victor in the games; while the presence of several young black rabbits bore witness that no colour prejudice existed in the rabbit world as yet. Sometimes, too, you would see the mother rabbit setting out with her young for a picnic in one of the beds of lilies—plants which always ranked as a great delicacy with them. . . . Certainly, from what one could see of them, one would have presumed that they belonged to a privileged species, and it was somewhat of a shock to find them classified as vermin.

My father, as I had expected, asked me to accompany him, and we set off at a great pace, so that I had almost to run to keep up with him. Fortunately I had by now fully recovered from my cigarette-smoking. He began at once explaining to me his revised plans for altering the north front and as he outlined the scheme his walking grew faster and faster, as always when he became excited about alterations to house and garden. From the brow of the hill he suddenly swung round, undid the binocular-case and clapped the glasses to his eyes. After examining the vast stone bulk of the house, he stabbed the air with his forefinger and said:

'There I propose to have two great erections. . . . What are you laughing at?'

Then he turned round again, examining the park through his binoculars, and the land beyond it, until, concentrating eventually upon a plantation of trees on the hill opposite, he remarked to me:

'To get the full effect of distance I'm afraid I shall have to fell old Taylor's clump over there.'

'But won't he object?' I enquired nervously.

'Really, I can't be expected to ruin all my plans just because an obstinate old man won't cut down a few trees. He'll be lucky, if only he'd realize it, because our woodsman will do it for him—I shall charge him nothing for the labour—and he can sell the timber.'

As we turned round to walk back to the house, the north front was suddenly illumined by the sunlight, which only reaches it in the late afternoon, and, even then, shines on it sideways, as it were. Nevertheless, its strength dispersed the tents of mist that still lingered on here, like gigantic mushrooms. Suddenly a breeze came and the great branches of the trees, oak, beech, and elm, fluttered their leaves on the air. Now the farmer's boy could be heard summoning the cattle to be milked, with a call that suggested a local adaptation of yodelling, and carried to a considerable distance. Soon he could be seen leading a line of cattle across the park to the home farm. The glory in the grass and in the trees would only last for a short while and then mists would come back to settle like great birds in the branches of the trees. We entered the house and crossed the hall towards the small garden door. The south front was as welcoming as the north was forbidding. Every object here glowed and the fragrance of stock, tobacco plant, and mignonette lay like a benison on the air.

# 3

## CIGARETTE ENDS

I T W A S two years later and I was eighteen, before my father
discovered that I smoked; he confined himself to delivering
a lecture to me every day for several weeks running upon the
perils of throwing away cigarette ends without first taking the
trouble to see that they were properly put out. From this he
went on to a dissertation about fireplaces. Such a pity, he
considered, that we did not still have a central hearth as they
did in medieval times, no chimneys to worry about, just a hole
in the roof, and no glass in the windows so as to give you
plenty of fresh air. . . . This advice—about taking trouble to
see that cigarette ends were put out—seemed unusually sensible.
Accordingly, I was very careful—more careful · even than
customarily—on the occasion when my father first took me
for a day or two to stay at Weston. Its lately deceased owner,
my great-aunt Lady Hanmer, had left my father as executor
of her will, and he had come here to discuss with a government
assessor the approximate values it was proposed to place on

certain objects in the house for the purpose of death duties. There was a heat-wave prevailing, a weather condition which seldom improves the temper, especially of Englishmen: but both men remained remarkably cool, when it is remembered that even in 1911, long before death duties had reached their present scale, they were regarded as iniquitous by those who had to submit to paying them.

My father at first took the assessor to be a rather rustic character, who would not be able to stand up to the full repertory of tricks, quirks, and tireless ingenuity to which he would be exposed, but he was soon forced to recognize that a worthy antagonist faced him. For example, when my father passed him a miniature to be catalogued, and suggested that the entry for it should read: 'Portrait miniature of old gentleman in white wig, wearing a blue ribbon', he examined it and said: 'I prefer to put: "Miniature on ivory of Lord North in wig, wearing the Order of the Garter." '

This was the first time I had stayed at Weston, which for a long while had been shut up, though I had once visited the house for the afternoon some six years before. That expedition remains unforgettable for several reasons—among them because it was the last horse-drawn jaunt in which I took part, albeit I was shortly to move more than ever before or since in equine society: but then my experiences could only be described as single-handed encounters with the brutes. (I was attached to a cavalry regiment and practised in the Riding School at five o'clock every morning all kinds of fancy-riding and still more obsolete Cossack tricks.) These encounters may have ranked as jaunts from the horse's point of view, but for myself could not be so described. No, this expedition was my last horse-drawn jaunt. . . . I was staying with two cousins at Bloxham some fifteen miles away, and when they heard that

View of Renishaw from the Steps of the Two Giants

View of the Lake and the Park, Renishaw

I had never been to Weston, though it had been in my grand-mother's family for over two hundred years, having always passed from mother to daughter or from aunt to niece, they decided I ought to see it. To reach Weston, which then seemed remote from anywhere, necessitated that I should make the journey in a hired wagonette, driven by the local carrier, with a face by Roger van der Weyden and bearing a name with a curious literary rhythm, for he was called Oliver Tendell Soames, which gave out a distorted echo of the name of one of my father's favourite authors. For what seemed long hours, we rolled down leafy lanes, the hedges in their first shrill unfolding forming almost a green tunnel. It must have been in late April 1905, and no drive could have been more delightfully out of its century. The houses in the villages all had thatched roofs and seemed to have remained in the late sixteenth century or even earlier, in the time of Brueghel the Elder. When at last we reached our goal it was nearly time to return, but not before we had seen some of the beautiful objects in the house, or walked in the garden which was then more full of wild flowers than of cultivated. There was a hollow at one side bordered by very old trees which was full of most fragrant white violets, and white, as well as speckled, maroon-coloured fritillaries, looking as if made of dyed shark-skin.

I had arrived there this second time in the month of May 1911. This visit was remarkable to me for different reasons from those which had governed my first glimpse of the house. My father sent Henry Moat down to the cellar to fetch one of the rugged, hand-made bottles of very old sherry. Henry soon returned with a dusty, cobwebby bottle which he had opened. My father said to him: 'Just pour yourself out a little and tell me if it is corked.' Henry accordingly sipped it; but his face, which at first registered a look of joyous expectation, changed

[33]

to one of raging disgust as he realized that he had carried up a bottle of home-made cowslip wine.

Impressed by the contents of the house, which seemed in a trance-like slumber undisturbed for centuries, I felt it was my duty to be more than ever careful about cigarette ends. One morning, however, my caution slackened and I threw a cigarette end on to the hearth. Then, realizing what I had done, I rushed across the room and stamped on the stump, still glowing, so as to be sure that it was quite dead, and placed it in a bronze mortar. My father watched me closely, but all I got for my trouble was the remark:

'So like your Uncle Francis!'

The tone of his voice made it quite clear that he was in no whit intending to express commendation. Both my father and mother always thus sought to place the blame on their children by referring to 'Your uncle' or 'Your aunt'. My father had always made it quite plain that he considered I ought only to inherit characteristics from his side of the family, while that any should come down to me from my mother's side ranked as Original Sin. . . . So I took refuge from reproach for an hour or so in the two fields beyond the garden. They were out of bounds for my father owing to his fear of hay-fever, which would certainly preclude him from following me, because these fields at this moment of the year were a paradise of flowers and flowering grasses; among these a profusion of cowslips and great clumps of various kinds of orchis with their leaves of moss-agate or green jade and their spikes of purple and gold and green and gold. . . . But now these flowers no longer appear because modern methods of farming have extirpated them as useless, in the same way that they have also banished the mushrooms which on September mornings used to be found here in such quantities.

# 4

## GOING FOR A DRIVE

'GOING for a drive' must not be confounded with and is a very different matter from a modern phrase with a certain similarity to it, 'being taken for a ride.' Indeed, it signifies its very opposite. . . . My first instinct when worried or unwell is still to go for a drive: a habit formed long ago in my childhood; though during the time that has elapsed since those days the actual process itself has changed almost beyond recognition owing to the supplanting of the horse by the motor-car, a development which has contracted the countryside. To drive ten miles then occupied the same time as it takes to travel sixty miles by motor-car today, so that all the points of pilgrimage in country I know well have had substituted for them other more distant attractions. The length of the drive was formerly one of its pleasures: to see over Hardwick, driving there from Renishaw some twelve miles away, made of the outing a day's excursion; whereas now it is just a jaunt of an hour or two. Moreover, when you have reached that splendid mansion you realize that its intense personality and beauty have similarly contracted and been spread thin. . . . To be 'taken for a drive' had a further significance. It often spelt convalescence from some childish complaint. . . .

We children were paying a spring visit to my grand-mother Sitwell when a bout of whooping-cough was identified —albeit our involuntary Indian war-cries must, one would have thought, have made its nature unmistakable. (Mean-while, during and after this bout, my father, I recollect, confident that he, too, had caught the infection from passing us children in the garden, could be heard defiantly whooping to—or at—the world from the seclusion of his study, though in the end the illness never developed and even at that time the sounds he made betrayed an air of artificiality and make-believe.)

When we, my sister and I, had sufficiently recovered, my grandmother would send us, attended by a governess, for a drive in the vivid and warm April of those days, through the deep, steep, leafy lanes, the hedges beginning to sing their first green canticles under the warmth of the sun and to show their first furry buds, or we would pass by marshy ground, at this time shimmering with white anemones or showing clusters of kingcups, their substantial knobs just breaking into glazed yellow flowers. We would roll along in the victoria driven by old Hill, my grandmother's coachman, through the heavy springtime, continually finding, it seemed, new roads to explore. Hill was celebrated for the slowness of his driving, and prided himself on a gift for carpentry and painting, and for his surly insistence on personally spoiling in odd hours my grandmother's finest pieces of furniture, however often he had been forbidden to touch them. He liked to cut down the measurements and proportions to suit his own rules of taste and

[36]

what he had decided was correct, and to paint what passed his rigid censorship in the colours in which he considered they should have been painted. . . . Sometimes for a change we would be taken along the chalk-white nudity of the Hog's Back to see Old Compton and the Watts Chapel, or to the church of St Martha, then we would return to Gosden, watching, as it grew darker, the golden and scarlet battles in the sky which heralded sunset and turned all objects, even the glittering white chalk churches, to a tone of gold.

'Going for a drive' in this slow fashion, however, hardly deserved its name and was more applicable to three other and more exciting occasions. One was confined to those weeks in the year which my grandfather Londesborough spent in Scarborough. The telephone had not yet come into its own, and a footman would come over with a message for my mother to say that 'His Lordship is going for a drive and would like to take the children with him.' So Edith and I, or one of us, would be waiting for him. He would soon arrive in his buckboard, which he drove himself—he was a celebrated whip, and his equipages were known for their elegance—and we jumped up beside him and started off. It seemed to take only a few minutes to be out of the town and bounding across the country-side to some prearranged spot on the moors, in Raincliffe Woods or Forge Valley, renowned locally for their beauty. In theory a groom should have been waiting three-quarters of an hour later at a particular place selected beforehand, to take the reins from my grandfather and enable the three of us to walk down through the woods to meet the buckboard again at a chosen spot. Usually we would reach it by way of one of the walks bearing the name of my mother or of one of her three sisters. The paths would be steep and full of damp green fern between the trees, while occasionally in this private part of the

[37]

woods we would find a rare wild flower, for example a burnet-coloured columbine. In time we would emerge out of the wood into the valley, as arranged, often to find that the groom had misunderstood his directions and had gone to the wrong place. Eventually, by some process of elimination, he would come upon us, but not before my grandfather had been given time in which to swear most imaginatively. His figure and his great height, as he walked up and down furiously, were most impressive and his beard imparted a certain iconic air to his appearance. However, as always, he was soon restored to good humour. . . . At another time he would take us through the bitter temples of the east wind to the cliffs. The few trees there were on this coast seemed to have been petrified in their flight away from the sea, albeit, to the contrary, the first indication of the spring was to be found here when in March the golden coltsfoot and celandines flourished in the rocky meadows.

The second exciting form of 'going for a drive' was when my mother would take us with her in a hired cab. She would be wearing her perfect country clothes which suited her simple beauty, and a bunch of sweet rose-geranium pinned at her waist. The cab would trundle us round down by way of the foreshore and the Marine Drive, then in course of being built. Great white wings of water, as if belonging to some extinct mammoth race of seagull, would swing up and fall with the thud of thunder on the huge squares of concrete that had been placed there as breakwaters, but which, against this background, nevertheless looked as small as a child's bricks. . . .

Most of all, 'going for a drive' meant to drive with my father round the twelve miles of green road he had made, doubling and redoubling round the hillsides of the Eckington Woods. After an early luncheon, we would set out in a

pony cart, painted green and yellow, drawn by a piebald pony
of smart appearance but uncertain age. It was common knowledge that he had spent several years in a circus, and he would
still, if he heard a certain tune played, begin to prance in circles
till it stopped. Even when passing through the territories of the
bluebell it was easy to imagine a spangled sylph on his broad
back, having alighted thereon from a trapeze. I have mentioned
bluebells. To my knowledge their beauty has no rival elsewhere. The beginning of May was here the best season for
them: then the whole ground became brighter and more blue
than the sky, and they filled the azure perspectives of the woods
with a delicate aroma which had in it, as well, a yeasty odour
as of newly baked bread. These ebullient groves and glades
seemed at first strange in country of such restraint, though in
truth it would reveal at other times, too, many dramatic
vistas of green precipice and sheer hillside.

My father would not himself drive, which, perhaps, owing
to the breakneck character of the woods, was just as well:
this drive was plainly one for a professional. . . . The bank on
one side was covered with mountain grass, growing like the
hair of nereids: on the other, you might obtain a brief glimpse
of the top of the dome of trees, now coming into their first
green splendour, or drive through a fragrant bower of wild
cherry in full flower. My father would not talk: his look was
abstracted—more than usually. Wearing a light overcoat and
a bowler hat, and sitting on his air-cushion, and with his
binoculars pressed to his eyes, he was surveying the prospect
which, as you went, unrolled a view of the hills opposite, as
when you are shown a Chinese or Japanese scroll. In his own
mind he filled these hills and valleys with architectural fantasies: there were temples and waterfalls and huge stone masks
from the antique world, through the mouths of which issued

the streams, stone boats on dams, and statues and smaller versions—pocket editions, as it were—of the Palazzo del Tè in Mantua, and canals which would lead from the lake to these valleys, so that coming here by boat you would avoid having to pass through the large village of Eckington and ignore the very existence of coal-mines in the neighbourhood. Indeed, as we drove round the woods, new ideas could be seen gliding like fish behind his rather pale eyes (though this was not how he saw his eyes himself, for it was during one of these expeditions, when we were returning and it was nearly dark, that a daddy-long-legs flew up into his eye, and he remarked: 'This has happened to me before. They mistake my eyes for stars.'). Though he had not yet grown his beard, his appearance was gothic and of the north. It matched this country, through which Robin Hood and his band had often roamed, no doubt, since these woods had once been part of Sherwood Forest, at that time of much greater extent than now. It was easy to picture him and his men, dressed in Lincoln green as a kind of protection, forerunner of camouflage, dodging from glade to glade. My father, however, felt little sympathy for them. Indeed, it was while we were driving through these same woods some years later that he had given me his opinion of the famous outlaw and his company. It was a very bad set for any young man to frequent, he warned me. Robin Hood—if he really existed at all—was always on the wrong side.

'I don't object so much to his robbing monks, who were no doubt bigoted and self-indulgent and thoroughly deserved it,' he explained, 'but he should have kept the money for the rich. Of course, it is true that there was no income tax in those days, still it was such a mistake to give the money to the poor, whereas the rich were the only people who knew how to spend it. They could always have found a use for it. Most selfish of Robin Hood not to have grasped that! You couldn't trust him. No, they were a very unpleasant set, I'm afraid,' he proceeded, 'and Friar Tuck and Little John were two of the worst in it, selfish and disreputable. I hope, dear boy, that you'll be careful to avoid the company of people like that.'

'Where should I find it?' I asked.

He ignored my question.

'Every young man,' he went on, 'should beware of joining up with such a party of crack-brained socialists. . . . As for Maid Marian, the less said about her, the better. She was obviously a bad lot. "Queen of the May", indeed! There can be no doubt that she blackmailed Robin Hood.'

'That's interesting. How did you discover it?' I asked. 'Where can I find an account of it?'

'We happen to know,' he replied, with a happy air of 'That's got you.' And he continued inexorably: 'I implore you to be careful not to mix with such people.'

# 5

## RECOLLECTIONS OF AN AWKWARD
## AFTERNOON IN KNIGHTSBRIDGE

THE air was—as indeed it should have been—Octobrine in its crispness and sweet odour, and brought the rustic smell of bonfires which could be seen burning brightly in smoky columns. But there was little to see of the flames at their centre, pallid in the sunshine. On the other side the window of the taxicab revealed the usual vista of bricks and mortar and at one point a cloud of dust swirling up in the near distance. For a moment the meaning of this eluded me, but I soon grasped its significance: it must mark the jubilant destruction of yet another of London's fine mansions—jubilant in intention, and no doubt in the expressive movements of the gang demolishing it, though the visual effect of the dust ascending to heaven was, to the contrary, depressing, as of smoke wafted from some biblical offering burnt in a clumsy attempt to propitiate an almost implacable deity. I paid off the cab and entered the dust-storm to find out exactly what was happening. . . . The diagnosis proved correct: Osnaburgh House with all its spacious, richly decorated rooms was in course of being pulverized to make way for office buildings and provide one more functional background in cement and plastic for the horde of bureaucratic typists who in the mysterious evolutionary workings of the twentieth century are plainly today the world's wonder and delight. Nearly asphyxiated, and at the same time turned to stone, I fought my way back to daylight, but not before I had recalled Osnaburgh House as it had looked for a ball given in June 1914.

At the very heart of that hot and dooming summer the guests had danced there to the rhythm of the famous waltz from the *Rosenkavalier*, the strains of which sounded in every London ballroom and were to return to many of the young men dancing that night as they lay a few months later dying of wounds in the barbed-wire thickets and rusty groves of No Man's Land. . . . By this time, the waltz, projected from so long ago—nearly two generations—was playing itself over and over again in my head as I walked away, until, growing tired of it, I experimented with the various remedies recommended to defeat this well-known affliction; curative measures such as deliberately substituting for the repetitive melody a verse or two of the National Anthem, thereby, as it were, indicating to the management that the concert was ended and the music must stop. But, in no degree discouraged, the waltz continued its beat unimpeded. . . . Then suddenly I forgot about it, as a memory of a different sort, but also connected with Osnaburgh House, asserted itself and took possession: those recollections of an awkward afternoon in Knightsbridge which give the title to these few pages—in brief, the incident I am shortly going to relate, the scene for which must have been pitched in the early autumn of 1917. . . . First, a few preliminary explanations are due to the reader.

When before the First World War my father came to London by himself for a few days at a time, his arrival evoked different responses from different people—for example, a member of one of the numerous firms of family solicitors he employed told me in later years that during the period of the visit, or, as he termed it, visitation, he would sit up the whole night through, with a cold-water bandage round his forehead, working out answers to some of the many legal conundrums that would soon undoubtedly shower upon him. . . . For my part, however, I would always in those early years try to find some entertainment or activity which might amuse or engross my father and thus leave him with less time in which to discuss with me my more salient faults and failings. This attempt at diversion was perhaps foolish since, as readers of my autobiography may remember, my father regarded all save purely esthetic pleasures as sinful (though, to boot, he would as wholeheartedly have rejected as sinful the conception of *sin* itself). But while he condemned amusement of any kind as dangerously self-indulgent, yet if in consequence no effort were made to provide it for him, he was inclined to be resentful. Moreover, the matter was difficult in other respects, too, because he would always refuse to see a serious play or a straight comedy, circuses were not in his line, and musical comedies did not appeal to him—though to this last there were exceptions, for he would exhibit something near enthusiasm for *The Belle of New York* and especially for the sweet singing in it of Miss Edna May. Miss Gertie Millar in certain roles had also been fortunate enough to win his approval. For the rest, *The Miracle* had interested him in 1911, and in 1880 he had enjoyed seeing on exhibition the giant, Chang. . . . Of him my father would often talk, telling us of how the Chinese colossus had been obliged to have a special Brobdingnagian chair made for him and that, though he measured eight foot two inches in height, he was so perfectly proportioned that himself did not so much appear gigantic, as cause those who had come to see him to look small, and my father would grow annoyed when I would protest that I liked a giant to be a giant, and that, withal, eight feet two inches did not seem so enormous: no, I was more interested in the idea of Og, King of Bashan, because not only did his height compel him to order a bed to be built measuring nine cubits by four, but tradition maintained also that he walked beside the Ark during the Deluge, that he lived to be three thousand years of age, and that when at last he died one of his bones was used as a bridge over a river. . . . Then there was, in addition, Anak to be considered, of whom the Hebrew spies reported that, compared with him in stature, they were but grasshoppers. . . . To my mind he was a more impressive mammoth, but he deserved special attention as the progenitor of a whole race of giants. Then, too, the claims of the monster Polyphemus must also be borne in mind. His skeleton had been dug up at Trapani in Sicily in the fourteenth century, so it was said, and showed him to have been some three hundred feet in height—there was a real giant for you! . . . All this, however, as my father did not hesitate to suggest to me, was beside the point, since there were nowhere any such giants on show today. . . . For the rest, it was useless to take him to a concert, since music—except his own singing, to which my mother had put a stop long ago—did not please him.

It was difficult: for example on one occasion in 1913 I had made a brave effort to amuse him. He dined with me first at the Marlborough, and appeared to be in tolerably good humour; thence I lugged him to the Hippodrome, to see the current revue, for which I had booked two stalls. No sooner had we settled ourselves in them than he began to entertain an aversion—no, that is too cordial a term—more accurately to form an instantaneous but abiding *loathing* for the principal members of the cast; a sentiment which he in no way sought to hide, or even to disguise. Whenever a single one of them appeared on the stage he would rock in his stall, move his feet about, fidget, fume, fuss, look up at the ceiling, sigh loudly, puff, and generally make moan. I suggested that we should leave, but he would not even quit his seat in the interval—when, I remember, he complained to me that the stars 'had no natural dignity or grace'—but insisted on enduring fretfully to the end. . . . The next morning he departed unexpectedly for Scarborough, where a day or two later he slipped the cartilage in his knee, had it operated on, but refused to be given any kind of anesthetic ('No one ever dreamt of taking an anesthetic in the Middle Ages. It is most self-indulgent'). And on being subsequently told by the surgeon not to move, but to lie still, he treated this injunction in so conscientious a manner that as a result he developed pleurisy and was confined to his bed for three weeks.

During this period he alleged that he suffered from insomnia; which led Henry Moat to remark:

'Naturally Sir George can't sleep all night as well as all day.'

But my father had determined to make use of valuable time that would otherwise be wasted, and explained, when I came on leave, and went to visit him in a nursing home, that he had spent the previous nights in experimenting with the various unusual positions in bed that he had found to be the most conducive to sleep. Of what might prove to be this valuable addition to human knowledge he had no intention of depriving the world. He sent for me the next morning and, when he heard my footsteps, called out to me:

'Come in at once, and shut the door. I've had an idea.'

'About sleeping?' I enquired.

'Yes. . . . The descriptions of my attitudes are difficult to follow in words alone, so I have decided to issue an illustrated pamphlet. I propose to call it *The Twenty-seven Postures of Sir George R. Sitwell.* Do you think that is a good title: will it sell the book, and whom shall I get to illustrate it?'

'Undoubtedly it will sell the book,' I replied, my mind first flying to the famous *Postures* of Aretino, then, more innocently, to the book of Lady Hamilton's Attitudes, and also to the parodying volume of caricatures which followed its publication. 'I will try to think of a suitable artist,' I went on, 'but there's so little of that kind of work being done at present. It's a pity Aubrey Beardsley is dead. It would just have appealed to him.'

My father looked pleased.

'By the way,' I continued, 'I tried one of your positions last night. It certainly helped me to sleep.'

'Which one?' he demanded.

'The one you told me about, where you lie with your nose over the edge of the bed. It's easier to remember than most of the postures.'

'That's *not meant* to make you sleep,' he snapped angrily. 'It's just to pass the time.'

In the end the book was never printed, though I did my best to encourage the idea. . . . At least, however, he found no difficulty in assigning the blame for the several misfortunes that had befallen him. 'It's all Osbert's fault for insisting on taking me to the Hippodrome and obliging me to sit through the whole performance.'

It had been an experiment plainly not to be repeated, and,

after war broke out, my endeavours to entertain him perforce stopped, until April 1916 when I returned to England and was posted to the Reserve Battalion at Chelsea Barracks, and then when from time to time my father, fresh from the ballistic dangers of Scarborough or the rigours of Renishaw, came to London, again I had to make some attempt to interest and amuse him. . . . No more theatres, and there were few private houses open—then I remembered the wall paintings by J. M. Sert in Osnaburgh House, and recollecting, too, my father's interest in the decorative arts, I wrote accordingly and asked if one afternoon I could bring him to see them. In reply, we were invited to tea the following Sunday.

We arrived together at four-thirty and found already gathered there a small party consisting of our kind hostess and a Mrs Brooke, to whom we were introduced in the customary English mode, rather vague and perfunctory, as well as to a few pieces of ordinary drawing-room furniture who remain nameless and faceless to this hour. Mrs Brooke, on the other hand, was definite in style, if rather tough-looking in a clerical manner—and moreover her face, under the accretions of time and of life at the Rectory in conjunction, seemed familiar, or at least put me in mind of someone with whose appearance I was familiar but of whom I could not for the moment seize the identity. . . . First our hostess conducted us into the Sert room, so that we could examine by ourselves the enormous wall paintings in sepia and gold of elephants, turbaned figures, and palm trees. . . . Sert, albeit not a great artist, certainly knew how to cover large stretches, and could be relied on to provide a sumptuous, smouldering background. Altogether in his span he must have painted acres and acres, nearly a square mile, of wall space. He was an artist who stood by himself in his century, having no rival and no one who

Great Drawing-Room. Family Group by Sargent and
the Renishaw Commode by Adam and Chippendale

The Ballroom at Renishaw. Brussels Tapestries designed by Leyniers
and executed by de Vos

wished to rival him. Since painting had moved away from drawing-room walls, he was now alone in his immense, two-dimensional, half-empty world of a lost Orient, fused of nostalgic, paranoiac visions of grandeur emanating from fancy-dress recollections of India, China, and Persia.

The others soon joined us in this room. . . . My father had been delighted with it from the first sight, and enchanted to find something new yet in no respect modern. Though by nature shy, he was on this occasion so greatly exhilarated that he talked freely. Directly he was in his place at tea he began a furious all-out attack on modern art, delivered with more gusto than he generally allowed himself. From painting he surprised me by divagating into the pastures of modern poetry —surprised me because he had never hitherto shown the slightest interest in that art or even a consciousness that it existed: but on the afternoon in question some magnet seemed to draw him relentlessly towards it. . . . He was just saying: 'Then there was that young man who died in the Dardanelles —I forget his name—they try to make out that he was a genius, but no good, no good, I can assure you,' when with a startling suddenness I realized *why* Mrs Brooke's face was so familiar— from photographs in the Press of Rupert Brooke: the resemblance was very marked; she must be his mother. I gave my father a good kick under the tea-table, but he did not even pause; only the as yet undreamt-of H-bomb could have stopped him. He went on: 'His poems were grossly over-praised in the Press.' . . . I could hardly believe my ears. Could it be true that this was really happening, or was it just a nightmare instalment of an instant in hell? Before, however, his memory could supply the missing name, the crowning horror was skilfully averted—but not before for myself, and no doubt for others, the sepia and gold elephants had begun to

[49]

climb the walls in earnest, and the palm trees wildly to wave their leaves in alarm.

'Sir George,' our hostess bravely intervened, 'you are sitting next Mrs Brooke, the mother of that wonderful young poet, Rupert Brooke. I *must* tell you, because,' she proceeded, drawing on her imagination, 'before tea you were just saying to me—but we were interrupted—how much you admired his work,' and continued, 'how different it is from the work of that other young poet—I, too, forget his name for the moment —of whom you were speaking.'

My father looked puzzled but said no more.

# 6

## CATCHING THE BUS

D EMOLITION has its triumphs no less than construction. The pulling down of Chelsea Barracks removes from London one of its most hideous buildings. Gone for ever is that dingy mass of dirty yellow brick with its air of solidity and its Byzantine or Romanesque arches, windows, and string courses of dull plum colour, gone for ever with its lost echoes of trumpet and drum and of the bugles that crowed the hours for one unpleasant task or another. All that remains of the colossal structure is an additional film of dust, such as that which fell at first on the doomed pleasure resort of Pompeii; a layer that covers the buildings in the vicinity and everything in them. . . . I was quartered at Chelsea during the first weeks of the war, from early August until the middle of December, when I went to the Front. Contemplating that time, the London scene seems effervescent though comparatively peaceful; but the chief impression which remains with one is that of the climate. It appears as if England always reserved a special kind of weather to serve as background for public catastrophes, and certainly there never was a finer summer or autumn than in 1914.

Examining the horrors of the Second World War, and before the coming of the Third now so plainly in preparation, the First World War has at its beginning the semblance of an old-fashioned panache about it. When you reached the Front, however, all ideas of chivalry and the like were swiftly dismissed by the universal stench, and by the sight of the pools of mud where whole companies of fat rats played at dusk.

Some incidents of that time remain in memory, and may be worth recording. . . . The war had swept down with great speed; but after a few weeks trench warfare had begun, and advance and retreat equally slowed down. Henceforth, for three years, an advance of a mere hundred yards was to cost thousands of lives, but this cessation of movement led many —why, no one will ever know—to believe that the war was ending. So many years had elapsed since the last European war had broken out—Balkan wars were endemic and not to be counted—that nobody knew quite how to behave or what to do. As a result, everybody recommended alternative and indeed opposite routes as the sole true road to victory. At one moment, for example, those who liked to talk about war with a pretension to strategic and tactical infallibility would advocate the immediate enrolment of every man and woman in the armed forces of the country, and the next, the same people would be advocating 'Business as Usual'. White Feather Trouble, too, had already begun though it was not to reach its apogee until about two years later. Meanwhile, these innocent-looking insults were nearly always offered to officers in plain clothes, or to young men under the age of enlistment.

Some of the most ardent and frenetic of these donors—in

almost every case a woman—had already begun to lay in a stock of white feathers for future distribution, but then came the difficulty of how to keep them in their original dazzling condition, since in the climate of London they were apt to turn buff in ten days, and black in a month, and somehow to present a buff feather did not seem quite the same thing as to offer a snowy-white plume. . . . Then there was the question of obtaining fresh supplies. Swans were too well able to break the arm or leg of anyone attempting to interfere with them; they must be ruled out absolutely. No, the only sure fresh supply was that to be obtained from the various kinds of seagull that in the winter gathered on the Serpentine, but even on a mild November day, if such came, nobody would wish to plunge into the water in order to pluck from the birds some white feathers. Moreover, if you attempted it, you were likely to get as good as you gave, for their cruel-looking beaks could inflict quite serious injuries. . . . The self-appointed distributors, too, wrote confusing letters to the papers, full of muddled advice and urging the joy and necessity of doing everything possible—including presumably the presentation of white feathers—for the lads who had joined up.

Shortly after the outbreak of the First World War I was sent down to the London Docks in command of the guard to be posted in various spots considered to be of some importance. I imagine we went to Tilbury, or perhaps Limehouse, for I remember long corridors between brick walls, with an occasional Chinese prowling or lounging about in the dark near-distance, for a black-out prevailed. I was also in charge of a large unused warehouse, used as an internment camp for—I was told—prominent enemy aliens who might prove dangerous. I was billeted in this building, which contained many chambers of little splendour but great size, and on arrival I

went round these halls to the accompaniment of stamping feet
and salutes from the armed guard. The rooms were crammed,
and the faces of some of the internees seemed familiar in a
vague sort of way. Out of their context, however, I could not
recognize them, until one man, who looked cheerful in spite
of the prevalent gloom and squalor, greeted me airily with the
words: 'Which table would you like tonight, sir?' Then,
suddenly, I understood. I was in charge of waiters of enemy
nationalities. It was terrible to be obliged to glare at them.
Already I had been shocked on the outbreak of war to hear of
the suicide of Max, the German hall-porter of the hotel in
which my father and mother always stayed when they came
to London. I had known him since I was a child. . . . But to
return to the warehouse—owing to the conditions in which
they were compelled to live, similar to those that had prevailed
in eighteenth-century Newgate—it was not long before
epidemics of impetigo and the itch, followed by many other
and no less attractive diseases, broke out, so that the formal and
rhetorical question which the officer going his rounds during
these men's dinners was obliged to put to them: 'Any com-
plaints?' came to have a new connotation, and one dreaded the
possible replies, giving in full detail the infections from which
they were suffering.

When after a few days the moment came for us to be
relieved we were relieved in more than one sense. Our footsore
successors arrived from Chelsea looking far from happy. I
recall that our march—or walk, as I preferred to call it in
military circles—had been long, hot, and dusty. Before starting
for home, I had just been reading several letters in the morning
paper from members of the civilian public who longed, they
averred, to make some sacrifice 'for the lads'. I was determined
to give them a chance of satisfying, even if vicariously, their

so patriotic craving. When, therefore, I saw a motor-bus approaching, I drew my sword, stood in the middle of the road, and stopped it. I then climbed aboard and explained to the driver and the conductor that I was commandeering the vehicle, that they were now to evacuate their present passengers and instead take my party back to Chelsea Barracks. They appeared to face the change with a certain happy insouciance. Not so the passengers. Though I pointed out that they now were afforded the opportunity of personally experiencing that which civilians were always writing to the papers to demand as a right, i.e. to make a sacrifice for the boys in khaki, they went with a bad grace. . . . My platoon was, of course, enchanted, and it was nice to look back as we went rushing on, and see the former passengers dragging along, mumbling to themselves or grumbling to one another.

When I arrived at Chelsea Barracks I found that in the few days in which I had been away a whole gang of senior officers, wearing on their tunics decorations which I at first mistakenly concluded had been the awards for bravery in the Crimean War, had materialized in the Anteroom. When the story of our exploit reached the Orderly Room these higher powers, of whom nothing had hitherto been heard in my lifetime, became much inflamed in their feelings, but they did not want to say too much about it for fear that other young officers would follow suit.

On returning, I found waiting for me, as so often, a letter of advice and discouragement from my father at Renishaw. He had remained there for some time and was still in a pacific —no, not pacific, but anti-the-current-war mood. In this letter he first took a whisk round the shops at which I dealt and emphasized the necessity for economy, so that if I were killed the next heir would not be too badly affected. He then proceeded to remind me of how the visiting General of whom he had often told me had come down from London to look at my father's regiment of Volunteers and had commended him in the warmest terms. The War Office had made a great blunder in disbanding that body, and the point was, could they ever recover what they had lost? The Territorials were not a patch on them, and Lord Kitchener's Army would also prove to be far inferior to these helmeted paragons. As for the statesmanship of politicians, it had been deplorable. 'Such a pity not to consult *me*.' The Emperor William was of a peace-loving disposition (my father felt some affinity to the Emperor William; they shared the same birthday, took the same interest in genealogy, the Middle Ages, and the gothic methods of torture, such as the Iron Maiden, the thumbscrew, and the iron boot). The German generals, most of them, were good fellows, more at home on the golf links than on the battlefield. . . . What had happened was that the Emperor William had suddenly found himself faced with the unexpected mobilization of Russian troops by a bloodthirsty Czar. Meanwhile the German blood was up. Nobody could wonder at it. The only certainty was that we could expect an invasion at any moment. Hollingworth was told to look out for suitable and remote retreats in which, when the Germans arrived, my father and his family could hide safely. Naturally they must want to capture him. When we moved at last to our house in Scarborough the raid on that town by the German fleet quickly followed and confirmed his worst suspicions. They must have been informed of his change of residence and were evidently determined to kidnap him, if only to obtain the benefit of his advice.

# 7

## HENRY MOAT

THE letters from Henry Moat that follow were addressed
to Maynard Hollingworth, then sub-agent at Renishaw.
Henry spelt his name in three different ways; in these letters he
signs himself 'Mouat', otherwise I have retained his original
spelling and punctuation. . . . Only three of these five letters
are dated. I have therefore placed them in the order in which
I presume from internal evidence they were sent. They all
clearly belong to his middle period of service before he left
in 1913 to be away for several years. The letter I print below
is dated July 7th 1905 and is certainly the first of the five in
a chronological sense:

Wood End, Scarborough.
I am much obliged to you for sending the boots so promply
they just arrived in nice time

I was much amused about the Old Clog he wants to shift out
of all business where a little expense is likely to occur but wants to

[57]

shine by keeping his accounts down and let everything go to pot but if it is not done he will have to sit up when we arrive I have a bomb or two. . . .

I should be much obliged if you would put a bed for Mr Pare in my bedroom over the pantry as otherwise the poor fellow will have (probably) to sleep in the barracks and as I always take care he has his food in the Housekeepers room and not in the servants Hall it would look out of place if he slept in the Barracks and had food in the Room

We had a fairly good camp the Sergt cook hung himself and three men got drownded

Trusting you keep well

I remain yours faithfully,

The Old Clog to whom Henry alludes was Charles Betts, who filled several posts at Renishaw, being responsible for the gardens and the woods. My father had at that time wanted some special trees planted and told Hollingworth to hand over the order to Betts. Betts planted something different and when my father complained, tried to throw the blame on Hollingworth.

Henry, as the reader will have grasped, had accompanied my father, who at that time commanded the local Volunteers, to camp. This body generally pitched its tents for a fortnight or so on the disused race-course above the town of Scarborough. If it were to rain, my father and Henry would always return for the night to Wood End. . . . My father was fond of relating how the General, sent down at the bidding of the War Office to inspect the Volunteers when they were carrying out an exercise—and when this hero was no doubt more or less fresh from the mixed bays and thistle-heads of the Boer War —had congratulated my father on his knowledge of strategy and tactics and had gone so far as to tell him that if only he had adopted the Army as a career, England might have had its own Napoleon.

The passage about Pare shows Henry's kind heart. Stephen Pare had been all but totally blinded by being struck by lightning and could only distinguish the difference between light and darkness. He had been with us for many years as odd man, employed at a pitifully small wage. Henry was anxious that he should be given his proper place in the very strict social hierarchy of the servants.

The Barracks was the dormitory in which the younger and less important menservants slept, a survival from the eighteenth century.

The second letter is not dated in full and I can find no clue to the year in which it was written.

> Wood End, Scarborough,
> Nov. 30th.
>
> For the love of Jasus stop sending anymore rotten apples the hampers cost 2/- coming the apples worth no more than 9d and a box arrived thursday I think and 6/- to pay Sir George was furious and wanted to know who ordered them to be sent perhaps you would find out
>
> Well we have Sir George laid up so I dont think he will be able to come to Renishaw for some time
>
> We are having ructions here I shake hands with myself when I find myself alive morn and even. I trust you are keeping well and having plenty of sport
>
> Well the best of good luck to you from your faithfully

The third letter is similarly dated by the month, May 18th only and no year is given, but it carries its own date in the last sentence. My father joined the Liberal Party in 1907.

Hotel Royal Danieli, Venise,

just a blast to say Sir Geo Lady Ida and Mr and Mrs Gray will be moored at Renishaw for a week from the 27th inst please inform Mrs Westby

an Italian chef will turn up about the 26th dont shoot him for Gods sake we want him I hope you are in the highest enjoyment of existence please have a good rest before we come because he gets up a(t) 5 o/c in the morning now my kindest regards to you. Sir Geo has turned a damned old radical good bye

The next letter is dated February 9th 1908.

Wood End, Scarborough.

I am all excitement and jumping about the gambols of a skittish young hippipotamas Well on friday next there is going to be a Grand Fancy Dress Ball and there is some young ladies going who I know are wearing skirts just long enough to cover their tea things

Well I should like to go but I have not got a fancy costume and suddenly thought if you would kindly take the great trouble to send me the coachman's (High Sheriff's) Livery Stockings and shoes not the overcoat hat or gaiters I should be so extremely grateful neither of the footman's would fit me but if you would kindly send the three pairs of shoes as I think the coachmans would be too big but I am not sure and it would be a pity if you only sent one pair I promise you on my word of honour I would send them back next monday Now do be a good fellow and send them

I hope you are in the pink of condition kindest regards

From yours faithfully

Readers of my autobiography may remember that Henry went to the ball in this livery and a white wig, representing, so he stated, Leonardo da Vinci. Indeed, a photograph of him in this fancy dress appeared in the pages of *Laughter in the Next Room*.[1]

The next and last letter lists the provisions that my father was taking to Renishaw for a flying visit (I can hear his voice announcing: 'I am going to run over to Renishaw for a few days' picnicking'). In preparation for this sprint, Henry writes to Maynard Hollingworth in January 1909:

> Wood End, Scarborough.
>
> Dear Maynard,
>     All been well Sir George and I will arrive at the——??? Hall tomorrow evening the train arrives GC 8.32 please send to meet us Brougham and heavy cart Sir George would like Hot Milk and bread the moment he crosses the threshold (please tell Mrs Westby Hot water bottle in his bed) Sir Geo will dine in the train
>     I am bringing 2 Chickens 2 Soles caviar Bacon plum Jam coffee apples Biscuits Rice Loin of Mutton Blanc Mange Flour tea and Mustard so will you please ask the good lady to order in the other things that she thinks is necessary
>     Trusting you are well
>
>> Yours faithfully
>> Henry Mouat
>
> P.S. Look out for a wire cancelling everything I will wire Mrs Westby if so. H.M.

Henry had devised through the years several techniques for dealing with my father. One—that of Infinite Patience—he used on this trip, when the following dialogue took place.

'Henry, the coffee wasn't properly made at lunchtime. It should be made in an earthenware pot and should be well stirred.'

'Sir George, it *was* made in an earthenware pot, and it *was* well stirred.'

[1] Page 41.

The point in the antecedent letter, however, which arouses the greatest curiosity is that my father should want 'hot milk and bread the moment he crosses the threshold'. It sounds as if it were a rite culled from the pages of *The Golden Bough* and referred perhaps to some obligation incumbent on the Priest-King in his last days of life before a knife of obsidian put an end to his term of office.

Maynard Hollingworth recently recalled to me some remarks Henry made to him about Major Viburne, for whom Henry cherished little regard. This paladin was disinterred from time to time and chartered by my father to oversee the household, muddle the accounts, and misorder the food. Major Viburne posed as a warrior and a gourmet, but in both instances his experience was limited. During the days of which I am speaking, for example, he was confined, by his own digestion, to a diet of dry biscuits, and he certainly never got nearer than Scarborough to any Front Line in the whole course of his long life. Maynard Hollingworth, then, said one morning to Henry:

'Is Major Viburne coming here this year, Henry?'

Henry looked round and said:

'I rather thought the gale last night would have swept him in, but I don't see him anywhere.'

On another occasion Hollingworth asked him:

'Did Major Viburne see much active service?' To which Henry replied:

'Yes, he fought right through the Canteen Campaign from beginning to end.'

Henry's talk was as uninhibited and as full of humour as were his letters. In his last period of service, many years after the foregoing letters were written, my father's restoration of Montegufoni was in full swing, and none of those who worked in the house could speak English. But Henry's sense of fun triumphed over lingual difficulties. Roars of laughter would come rolling up the stairs from the servants' quarters. The same outrageous robustness of expression still marked his conversation in his broken Italian, no doubt as much as in English. Nothing about him was much changed. Only the sound of his footsteps had grown a little heavier, indeed everything about him had grown a little heavier than in earlier years. In short, he had remained essentially himself, but an expanded self.

Other characteristics marked his talk as well as individual humour. He proved, withal, to be a repository of rough wisdom and of local—as will be seen in a moment, of more than local—lore and was apt to use phrases and turns of speech of forgotten derivation. . . . Thus, in *The Scarlet Tree,* I mention that, looking up at a blue sky with huge white clouds moving in stately progress across it, Henry referred to them as 'them great big Norwegian Bishops'. . . . A few weeks later I received a letter from Australia in which my correspondent, who had just read the book, wrote of the phrase suggesting that the epithet *Norwegian* afforded an ineluctable clue. In Norse mythology, he went on to say, the souls of the dead are represented as bees and were supposed to traverse the sky in what was specifically termed a 'beeship' (*bÿskip*): of which *Bishop* was clearly a corruption. He added that to find the phrase still lingering even in a mutilated form in popular speech constituted a survival of considerable romantic interest. Whitby, which always had many dealings with the Scandinavian countries opposite, remained the centre of Henry's universe, and he always bore with him a blast of nautical air, with the particular tang of the North Sea in it.

[63]

## 8

## JEZEBEL HOUSE AND A GRAND
## PIANO

AT SCARBOROUGH in the winter the incessant roar of the
sea, the salt spray that stung the face far inland, the bitter
cries of wheeling and pouncing gulls, the attitudes of the bare
trees, caught, as it were, in the very act of flight, all seemed
designed to create and maintain an atmosphere of power,
tension, and of actual terror. For weeks together there would
be no break in the tragic estimate thus presented. Howbeit,
in the spring and summer months the prim, trim terraces,
crescents, and gardens, full of dogs and flowers, appeared to
offer a setting for comedy and even for farce rather than for
tragedy. In summer tragic events were nevertheless apt to
occur, and the mysterious happening which follows I relate
here in example of them—though I write of the episode as my
memory records it and not from any recent studying of the
columns of contemporary newspapers.

My grandmother Sitwell, a delicate old lady of determined
and active philanthropy, had many years before, with the aid,

I think, of the Bishop of Hull, established a Home for 'girls of a certain class'. In the repulsive refuge to which these sad Dickensian creatures were consigned, Jezebel House, the matron gave them boots and dresses that served for a prison in themselves and further, as a perpetual corvée, they were compelled to do laundry work. Their resentment at the ungracious way of living they were obliged to follow found easy expression in many a shredded shirt and ripped chemise. . . . Jezebel House itself was a square, red-brick building, doubly fenced and set back behind an inappropriate palisade of thick wood—inappropriate because it seemed unnecessary from the look of it to enforce any more the sense of restriction. Yet, in spite of its plainness, the atmosphere of the building, with its windows glaring coldly above the fence, was not so much gloomy—that was to be expected—as sinister, and I used to notice how often this house associated itself in my mind as the background for any story of crime or mystery which I might be reading: *Dr Jekyll and Mr Hyde*, for example.

At some time during the First World War Jezebel House was shut—shut perforce, since the professional had now begun to make way for the amateur, and in consequence the former kind of occupant was no longer so easily to be found. For the later long years of war, and even for a few years of the peace that followed, the square building stood deserted and dusty. The agent in whose hands the sale of the property rested was a man prosperous, well known and respected in the town, and very regular in his habits and hours of work. Therefore, one day, when he did not return at the usual hour to his home—his house was in the centre of the borough—it seemed so very unlike him that after a little while his wife rang up the office, only to be told that he had left it some hours before. The family began to grow more and more alarmed as the minutes went by without any sign of him, and at about nine o'clock his sons went out to start a search. The evening was still light and clear with that very logical, hard summer-evening light of the north. First they visited several empty houses included in their father's lists, thinking he might have taken a client to inspect them, and last among them they called at Jezebel House. They penetrated the wooden barrier, the gate of which they found unfastened, though the front door of the house was locked. Its windows were shuttered and all was quiet, so they decided not to enter but to return home.

From the first his family had been afflicted with an indefinable, irrational sense of disaster, and now, knowing that sleep was impossible, they determined all of them, mother and sons, to stay up. So they remained in the sitting-room which faced the street, waiting hour after hour in absolute silence, for they were too perturbed to talk, and in English seaside towns life used to die early in the evening. Indeed, they sat there until at last the blackness of the sky began to lift a little and the electric-light globes still burning in the room called out beyond the square window-panes an indescribably pure and luminous tone of blue. . . . In these noiseless and innocuous moments before the dawn, at last a curious sound reached them—the sound, it seemed, of something being dragged along outside —and there followed a distinct scratching at the door. All of them rushed to open it, and a heavy, dark body crawled over the step into the lighted room, creeping along on all-fours like an animal. He was charred almost beyond recognition—so badly injured that not even the members of his own family could understand what he said. He had no coat on, but in the hospital to which he was at once taken they found his gold watch, which he usually wore in his breast-pocket, in one of his trouser-pockets. . . . During the few days he lived he tried

[66]

many times to make himself understood, framing the same words over and over again. At last, only just before he died, they seized the purport of them: '*Jezebel House*'.

The police acted immediately and had the house searched. They found the door still locked on the inside. All the windows were shuttered and bolted. Finally they broke the door open and in a room on the ground floor at the back found the electric light burning. The dead man's coat was hanging on a chair, but they could find no sign of violence, nor of anything having caught fire. The nature of the crime which must have occurred there defied every subsequent attempt at elucidation.

At Scarborough the trim, prim terraces, crescents, and gardens, I was maintaining, seemed in the springtime and summer months to offer a field for comedy and even for farce rather than for tragedy. Singular incidents were always liable to occur there—for example, a few years earlier there had been the episode of the bath and my great-aunt Lady Hanmer, an octogenarian widow whom I have described at greater length[1] elsewhere, so that all I need say about her now is that she lived —had elected to live—near the station in a house built of ugly yellow brick, that she had a genial and ample presence, and to remind the reader of her many shawls, of her eyebrows, or sometimes of just one, lightly painted in—like a sketch for an eyebrow rather than an eyebrow itself—and of the accompanying painted fringe above her forehead, over which was balanced an elaborate cap of lace and ribbons of baby pink and blue. We—my brother and I—had always seen her in one position, seated in an armchair near the fire, in a drawing-room

[1] *Left Hand, Right Hand!*, Vol. I, pages 167-9.

[67]

filled incongruously with eighteenth-century French furniture. For us, in memory, she seems to float, very fully swathed, above the smoke from passing trains, as, in an earlier age, patrons were portrayed posturing in apotheosis on rosy clouds on ceilings.

After the manner of the lives of all other human beings, however, Lady Hanmer's life knew more intimate moments, and it was in one of these that she found herself tightly wedged into her bath, and quite unable to rise from it unaided. The door, of course, was locked. . . . She managed by shouting, after half an hour or so, to attract the wandering attention of a young housemaid, who at once ran to inform her superior of their mistress's plight; together, they proceeded to force the door. When they had entered, each took one hand, and pulled and yanked, but all of no avail: Lady Hanmer remained recumbent in the bath, nor, though they tried by pouring in more water, could they float her. They hauled again, but there was no sign of getting her loose—in short, the old lady was too heavy for them. Consulting together, they agreed that it was a man's job to extricate her—but how could a male be introduced into the room without indecency? This constituted indeed a problem; a choice between a breach of the prevailing moral code and a life occupancy of the bath. It was decided that at all costs Lady Hanmer must be restored to circulation. . . . Presently, Wilkins, the head housemaid, had a startling and ingenious idea. She and Emily sought Gimlet, the butler, who had been in Lady Hanmer's service for fifty years, and explained the predicament. Then, no doubt with some vague echo of the Judgment of Paris in their heads, they blindfolded him, tying a black bandage across his eyes, lest perhaps he should cry 'Mine eyes dazzle!' as did the Duke at sight of his sister in Webster's *Duchess of Malfi*. Together the two women led him into the bathroom, where the old lady, placing one hand delicately in

[68]

his, was drawn to her feet. He was then ceremoniously conducted down to the hall, where sight was restored to him. . . .

But this was only one unusual incident: while the fact that my father had seven times been a parliamentary candidate for the borough, and had in consequence called on every voter on at least seven different occasions—for those were the days of a more limited franchise and a personal visit was expected from each of the candidates—provided still more and wider opportunities for comedy; because in consequence we possessed innumerable friends and acquaintances of every sort in the town, and among them are two I must describe for the unfolding of this episode. . . . One of them, Sister Dorothy, was an acquaintance more than a friend, though circumstances forced us to see her often. For several years she had been in charge of Jezebel House and when that establishment shut she settled herself comfortably on my religious Aunt Florence, who had, most conveniently, just become a permanent invalid. Sister Dorothy was middle-aged and buoyant. In appearance she seemed positively bursting with ill-health, though she contrived in the end to live to be eighty; except for the tea-fiend's protruding teeth, her face looked as if it had been roughly thumbed into shape out of an overripe tomato. Perhaps because she was a member of some Sisterhood vaguely affiliated with the Church of England, and in order to stress her almost official status, she always dressed after the pattern of a travestied nun.

Miss Susan Tugworth, the other person I have to describe for the purpose of what follows, was a real friend, whom I can remember from a very early age. My mother and the rest of the family were very fond of her and she had become a figure in the house, my mother often employing her on various errands in which tact, trustworthiness, and a knowledge of people in the neighbourhood were required. . . . I first recollect the figure of Miss Tugworth when she came to teach me how to write the letter 'S', pointing out to me that it was shaped like a swan. I still recall my efforts to make it look like one, and how the view outside was, appropriately, everywhere of swan's-down, because snow was falling and covered everything, even the trees, with white, soft feathers. Miss Susan, the eldest of her family, was kind and sad and overworked, never from the weight of any particular job, but from the drift and variety of the small burdens which she had assumed, the different kinds of task which she had been obliged to undertake in order to earn a living for herself and her drove of sisters. They were in a genteel way bitterly poor, and lived in a small white house which had belonged to their father, an artist of some repute, known in his day for his pictures of tall, slender, and beautiful women, carrying on their shoulders Grecian water jars or posed among almond blossom and peach. By a mysterious decree of fate, however, he had drawn as his allotted share of children only the very opposite of the type he liked to paint. These sisters, stunted, short-legged, long-bodied, their drawn-out, dog-like faces blue with cold, were all of them charming in their own way—that is to say they had charm, but not of the sort which he would have appreciated. Now he was dead, some of the daughters had married, and others had settled down to being invalids. It had devolved, therefore, on Miss Susan to support the afflicted. She remained patient, with an air of almost amused resignation and humility before the successive tricks of destiny. . . .

At the time of which I am writing, the First World War was over and my father was again filling our Scarborough house with miscellaneous objects he had bought in Italy, and was pouring them into Renishaw as well: which, however, was large enough to absorb the contents of many vans. Not everyone appreciated their esthetic effect, for the English taste is both more sober and less funereal. Thus Henry Moat plainly felt a distaste for these gimcrack but imaginative pieces. He was wont to say of them—as he did, too, of my father's alterations and decoration of rooms—'Everything for show, and nothing for convenience.' If it had been left to him, all would have been of good, sound oak.

In a letter to Hollingworth he writes:

. . . Sir Geo arrives monday at 2 oclock and would like you to have the cases unpacked in the morning already for him to go through I am going to ask him if he will allow me to go through them after him with a huge hammer.

My father used to get very worked up about the disposition of the objects, and it tempted him to rope other people in and obtain their opinion. During one of these expeditions, he was in the drawing-room at Renishaw supervising the unpacking and instructing two workmen, telling them how to convert two altar vases of gilded wood into paraffin lamps. Henry walked in, carrying something for the rooms beyond, and my father called out to him:

'Henry, don't you think these will make excellent paraffin lamps?'

'No, Sir George, I don't,' was the answer.

My father added: 'Then you're quite mistaken. They will.'

Whatever may be the true estimate of the objects, they continued to arrive for some twenty years, except between 1914 and 1918. Fresh loads of gaily ramshackle furniture, painted and gilded chests, tables and chairs, or cabinets gone to

[71]

the other extreme and blacker than black would come from Naples, Palermo, Florence, Rome, and Venice, bringing with them more than their fair portion of woodworm and death-watch beetle. A few years later, it is true, my father sent back most of these pieces of furniture to Italy: but at the moment they led to Wood End being very crowded. A consequence of this was that one morning my mother sent for me to her room and said:

'The lumber-rooms, as usual, are getting much too full and I think I shall sell the contents of the first of them at the top of the stairs; not that there's much in it that will fetch anything —though there's an old piano that might sell.' After a moment's pause, she added: 'It's curious, I don't remember seeing it before. Don't say a word to your father or he'll only make a fuss. . . . I'll let the auctioneer know and he can perhaps take the things away next week when your father goes to Renishaw for a few days.' . . .

They were duly moved, and in time the auction took place, bringing in some seventy pounds odd, of which the piano accounted for six guineas. (It was one of those recurrent moments when to sell a piano brings in little, while to buy one costs a fortune.)

What my mother had *not* known was that Sister Dorothy had, a short time before, received as a legacy a piano which proved too big for her to house, and that she had therefore asked my father to shelter it for her until she could contrive to find for it a permanent home. My father, who liked her for her practical common sense, as he termed her lack of imagination, and also, perhaps, to be different, had consented. The instrument had duly arrived and had been carried straight up to the lumber-room while my mother was out.

At some moment within the following fortnight my father

must have received a letter from Sister Dorothy to say that she had at last bought a house in which her brother would live and where she could join him on her retirement. She could, therefore, now have the piano—on which I may add that neither of them could, perhaps fortunately, play a note—and accordingly a van would call for it. My father did not mention the matter to anyone—he saw no need to—but when the van arrived and the men were sent upstairs to the lumber-room to remove the piano and found nothing there he rushed into my mother's room and said without a previous explanation:

'Where is Sister Dorothy's piano?'

Though this was the first my mother had heard of its ownership, she immediately grasped the situation. Not, however, realizing that the van men were in the house, she said, in order to gain time and because the kindly Miss Tugworth had always solved so many difficulties for her: 'I think Miss Tugworth must have got it.'

My father tore out of the room, saying:

'I never heard of such impertinence—to remove a piano without even consulting *me*!'

He then rushed downstairs, spinning like a tornado, and directed the van men to Miss Tugworth's house. . . . The door was opened by one of her sisters, and before she had time to reply four men in green-baize aprons had entered. They strode by instinct straight into the drawing-room where poor Miss Susan Tugworth was sitting alone in a heavy coat, enjoying its brittle, cold splendour. This room was one of the few possessions of which the whole family felt proud. It had stayed as it had been left by their mother, full of spindly bamboo tables and useless knick-knacks, small shoes in silver, and heavily cut glass scent-bottles with silver stoppers. It also exhibited a grand piano, which had not been played upon since their mother's

[73]

decease. . . . Going up to the piano, the apparent chief of the gang playfully struck a note and said: "E told us to take it away.' (Obviously the van men had been impressed by my father's considerable personality, for not one of them ever referred to him directly, but as though his name were taboo, because sacred, alluded to him as "E' or "Im'.) The other three men now advanced inexorably on the piano, and together they whisked the heavy instrument out of the room. It was a scene which, to look back on, might have been invented by the contemporary Kafka. Miss Tugworth kept on saying weakly, over and over again: 'You can't do that,' to which they would reply:

'Oh yes, we can. 'E told us to take it away.'

'But it's *my* piano.'

'That's not what 'E says. It's by 'Is orders.'

'Who is "He"? '

''E said you'd know 'oo 'E was.'

Poor Miss Tugworth, so kind and pliant! The van started and carried away her piano to embellish and make genteel Sister Dorothy's new house. Several days passed before Miss Tugworth could even find out where the instrument had gone, or who had given the order for its removal. Whether she ever received it back again I cannot recall: only that she laid no blame on anyone. My mother, on the other hand, was furious with Sister Dorothy and retired to bed for a week, and no one for many years was allowed to mention the word *piano* in her presence.

# 9

## THE ADVENTURE OF THE PHANTOM
## TAX-INSPECTOR

IN THE dining-room at Renishaw there hangs among the
assembled portraits one which was not there when I was a
child. It is not a work of art: in fact the tortoiseshell frame
which contains it is responsible for any effect that it contrives to
make; nevertheless it is plainly—I fear *plainly* is the precise and
operative word—a painstaking, and a painsgiving, likeness. It
represents a young girl, who carries perched on the crook of her
left arm a rather mean-looking and curiously undecorative
green parrot. The girl herself wears on her slightly smug,
round face an expression of insipid, innocent surprise; I
apprehend that she would look even more astonished could she
be aware of the circumstances attendant on the last purchase
of her portrait and its reappearance in this house. . . .

We must, since one thing leads to another, begin at the
beginning, or even before it, and touch on matters seemingly
unconnected with it, but which in reality shaped the course of
small events which led to its acquisition—events which though

minute in themselves are part of the chains and fetters of the inexorable law of cause and effect. . . . During the winter of 1920–1, then, the door of the house in which my brother and I lived in London could be seen to lack its knocker for a period of some three months, and any friends of ours passing would have been able to interpret the message which its removal carried; for in the same way that the presence of the Sovereign in a city is made evident by the flying of a Royal Standard over his palace there, so, albeit obversely, the taking down of the knocker from the door of his sons' house signalled to those in the know that my father was in London. In addition, if they went by frequently, they would have comprehended that he was paying a longer visit than was his wont. The explanation of the periodic disappearances of this object was that I had found it in a lumber-room at Renishaw, where it had reposed for years: it must have come from Italy, is made of bronze, and its shape—that of a ring slightly pulled out at the sides—is formed by two dolphins, face to face, fin to fin, their entwined tails closing the circle. Seeing it, I at once grasped how well it would look on the door, which, at the time of writing, it still embellishes, and took it to London without revealing to my father that I had done so, for though he had several years previously handed Renishaw over to me, he yet liked to be consulted, and I knew from experience that the words which came most easily to his lips were 'No, certainly not!' or, with a note of warning in his voice, 'Oh, I *shouldn't* do that if I were you!'

All those dreary long winter weeks, therefore, I was obliged to conceal the knocker, my father having sought refuge in London for reasons which I will shortly disclose. . . . In the days of which I write, Scarborough, ancient and historic borough, and modern pleasure resort, yet retained a

[76]

marked character of its own. . . . Many incidents of past years there I could relate: and, though varied, they would be equally grotesque. Of them all, the Adventure of the Phantom Special Commissioner of Inland Revenue is perhaps the most exceptional—as unexpected as the episode in London to which, by causing my father to spend the winter there, it led up. In those days we still had a house in Scarborough—Wood End—always referred to by a writer in the local Press as 'Sir George and Lady Ida's marine residence'; a description which ever summoned to mind the image of some submerged and finny grot at sea bottom with huge fish darting in and out in strictest privacy: the words certainly served to make the place sound cool and remote. However, Wood End was not so isolated or lonely as the description suggests. Several taller houses overlooked its rectangular block, built of dark, golden stone, set in a large garden and within range of all the sea's voices, its roarings, its tremendous thunder and lion-voice threats, its occasional purring and light-hearted delusive promises.

It was some time during the late summer that my father first noticed one of the Special Commissioners of Inland Revenue, so he asserted and continued to maintain, skulking on the roof of the nearest house, observing him through binoculars. My father declared him to be a dignified-looking individual, wearing striped trousers, a morning coat, and a tall hat—no very suitable garb, I reflected, for someone literally 'on the tiles', who must wish to escape attention. Apparently the stranger stood there for hours, patiently watching Wood End. At the beginning my father was furiously angry, and would stare back through the spy-glass which he always carried about with him when at Renishaw or Wood End, so as to be able to 'obtain the distant view'—in other words, in case he should see a chance of knocking down some building, and beginning to erect another in its place. . . . I was never able myself to discern the mysterious stranger, and my own feeling was that he must be either my father's Narcissus-like *doppelgänger*, a projection from and of his own personality such as Edgar Allan Poe was concerned with in his story of *William Wilson*, or else that victim of *delirium tremens* who had lived ten years before—and apparently was still living—in the house in question. From time to time the prey of the most oppressive alcoholic nightmares, he was probably—if it were he—scanning our garden for stray pink elephant or undulant boa-constrictor; but my suggestions to that effect were contemptuously rejected. No, my father had guessed the identity of the prowler immediately, and once and for all. He did not believe in ghosts, but with his whole being he believed in the existence of his Special Commissioner. Nothing could shake him. When I said to him: 'How can you be so sure that he is one of the Special Commissioners of Inland Revenue?', he resorted to the use of one of his favourite and most irrefutable replies:

'*We happen to know.*'

The phantom continued to haunt him, so he decided to go away. He would not visit Renishaw as my guest, for the insolent intruder might follow him there, hide in one of the stables or outhouses, and steal out unobserved, to watch and follow and pry, and, in fact, like the hosts of Midian, to 'prowl and prowl around'. Instead, he took the lease for the autumn and winter of a furnished apartment on the sixth floor of a block of flats in Knightsbridge: at least there he would not be over-looked, and would be free from the daily persecution—as he had grown to regard it—that he had suffered at Scarborough.

So it came about that my door remained for several long months without its customary knocker. . . . From his new and

[78]

temporary eyrie my father could pursue his many interests: he could be seen—if the Commissioner in question had followed him—wearing frock-coat and silk hat, the well-known air-cushion like a lifebuoy on his arm, leaving the building every morning for the Reading Room of the British Museum, where he was at last in the final round of a long hand-to-hand tussle with the Grosvenor pedigree. He was, however, no longer attended to the door by Henry Moat, now superseded by my former soldier servant, the nimble Robins. . . . Though the conduct of his life followed its customary course in London, the experiences of the last few weeks had left him in a more than usually suspicious frame of mind. When, therefore, he received a letter from a stranger, asking him to visit his house, my father's reactions were mixed (the Commissioner again?). The correspondent claimed to be an ex-naval captain, lived somewhere at the top of Hampstead Heath, and had written to say that he had lately purchased at a sale a small portrait which had formerly hung at Renishaw, and depicted a Sitwell ancestress as a child. He never sold—he proceeded to write—anything he had bought, but on this occasion would like to make an exception and offer the picture to my father. He would be at home on Tuesday afternoon, and could show the painting.

This letter at once excited my father's predominant interest —in family history—but also roused his latent fear that, since his life was of such great importance to the country, someone might attempt to kidnap him for ransom, or even to kill him. (He used, I cannot imagine by what means, to acquire certain slang phrases, and I recall him saying, in this connection, 'I fear that one of these gangs may bump me off!') There had been that odd incident, he recalled for my benefit, of the sample of cocoa that had reached him through the post, addressed in handwriting unknown to him (he had caused it to be put on the fire at once, but even then it had burnt with a curiously coloured flame, and had made a spluttering noise). But at whatever cost to himself, he intended to inspect the portrait (which would it prove to be, Katherine Sacheverell who had married George Sitwell, or Francis Sitwell's wife, or Mary Reresby? much depended on that); there was no point, however, in incurring needless risk, so he would take with him Robins, who could carry a harquebus—what did they call it now?—of course, a revolver! Robins no doubt would require considerable coaching beforehand in how to act and how to handle the weapon, but my father would give him a few hints, so he could not go far wrong.

The instructions which Robins received were that he was to sit beside the driver, to draw a revolver ostentatiously from its holster directly he arrived outside the house, and, when my father alighted, was to remain holding it in an obvious and menacing manner, at the same time lolling to show he felt no fear himself, till my father should give a signal. (My father said he would know by the atmosphere of the house after he had been in it for five or ten minutes what course of action to follow. If all were well he would make certain faces and gestures, which he had previously taught Robins to interpret, from a window or possibly from the garden: if he failed to appear within a quarter of an hour Robins was to fight his way in at the point—or, rather, at the barrel—of his revolver—for if the owner were really an ex-naval officer he might be a good hand with a cutlass.)

The day came, the taxicab was hired. The driver, however, at first objected to Robins sitting beside him, protesting that it was contrary to the law that governed the life of taxicabs, but as soon as he saw my father in tall hat and topcoat, with a collar

The Dining-Room, Renishaw

Staircase at Renishaw

of Irish beaver, a fur which he claimed to be extinct (and it looked to me as if the allegation were justified), the driver's objections were overcome, and they started on their singular quest. They arrived, and the house seemed an ordinary, rather pretty Hampstead dwelling. My father rang the bell and the door was opened almost immediately by a neatly dressed parlourmaid. Robins, therefore, watched the house and garden with anxious attention and was relieved, after some eight and a half minutes had passed, to see my father's face grimacing at him from a shrubbery just the other side of some oak palings, and to read its message and that of the accompanying gestures: 'All Clear'.... What the ex-naval officer—who proved to be of a well-known type, bluff, hearty, adventurous, and intelligent —can have made of the highly unconventional behaviour of his visitor, who in every other respect seemed so dignified and courteous, we shall never know. The taxi-driver, for his part, from whom some reaction might have been expected, did not seem in the least astonished: he commented, as my father got out: 'Nice gentleman, that, quite of the old school,' but certainly my father, with his beard, as he had signalled across the fence from among the speckled laurels, laburnums, and privets of a suburban garden, must have looked rather strange, unusual today as a satyr in a glade. The adventure had, it is true, a happy ending—no one was killed; my father left the house with the picture under his arm, the ex-naval officer had acquired the twenty-five pounds he had asked for it, and in time I was able to restore the door-knocker to its accustomed place. Nevertheless, the expedition had left a tender spot in my father's memory, for when one day, some years later, I began to question him about it, he gave me a severe look, and said:

'Don't ask silly questions, dear boy.'

# IO

## LA GALLINA

WHEN the Campanile of St Mark's had but lately collapsed, the Saint on his pinnacle landing from the air in so gentle a manner, as if knocking at the great doors of the cathedral in order to crave sanctuary, and by this unique gesture of abdication had given back to the golden church and to the Piazza their ancient and proper proportion, my father went to Venice to meet Signor Bracciaforte, so that with the aid of this expert he might try to find and buy for Renishaw a pair of garden statues and a fountain. That they should be fine and beautiful works of art was all the more important because he relied on architectural rather than horticultural features for his effects. Flowers, in fact, were only admitted to the garden if innocuous and indeed insipid enough not to attract attention to themselves. In short, he hated strong colours, and in this connection a friend recalled to me one more instance of it. . . . Ernest de Taye, for very many years head gardener at Renishaw, but at the time of which I write new to the job, asked one morning to see my father. He obtained permission, entered my father's study, and said to him in his soft foreign voice—he was a Belgian from Ghent:

'Sir George, I am sorry to inform you that the large very brightly coloured rhododendron near the fern-leaf beech was blown down in last night's gale'—only to receive the to him startling reply:

'All I wish is that it had been blown right out of the garden!'

It will be appreciated, therefore, to what a degree my father had to depend on the more permanent and organic features of a garden. The best examples of statuary of the kind he sought were to be found scattered over the former Venetian territories on the mainland. Accordingly, my father and Signor Bracciaforte set off at eight or eight-fifteen of a morning either to worry and beat down the dealers in Venice itself or to ransack throughout the day one of the neighbouring little cities.

Here I must turn aside to establish the character of Signor Bracciaforte. I have written of him elsewhere, that he was the Pécuchet to my father's Bouvard. My father always referred to him not as a dealer of perspicacity and principle, but as 'our little artist friend', and it was true that before becoming a dealer he had been a painter. Indeed, to that very day he continued to see life in terms of Murger's *Vie de Bohème* and still wore a beard as a declaration of his faith, though it was a rather thin and token beard. Nevertheless, all that he lacked in order to complete the costume of the part was a floppy brown velvet beret. Born out of wedlock, Bracciaforte was the warm-hearted offspring of a peasant woman and an Italian Count, who had seen her working in the fields. He had married an Englishwoman who had a fortune of her own, but he continually looked to left and right. He was kind and gay by nature, and a creditable human being, though one not lacking in absurdities and contradictions. He loved nature, and liked especially birds. His English was a language fluent but consisting of words which were unidentifiable, and he would deplore for many minutes at a time—and choosing my sister as audience—the character of the cuckoo as a mother, always beginning: 'Miss Edit, have you tor' what it min . . . ?' (Miss Edith, have you thought what it means . . . ?)

I saw him last in 1949, at the age of ninety-three, when he suddenly materialized with a suitcase and a niece, who deposited it and him at Montegufoni. Unexpected things had happened to him during the war years. His pictures, painted sixty years before, had suddenly become the favourites and paragons of the advanced Italian painters of the day. Articles had appeared in the papers demanding the facts of his life and death. Nobody knew, of course, that he was, or could be, at such a great age, still living; so his fame was posthumous in his lifetime. His house (his wife was by then dead) had been commandeered during the war, and well though he knew the city, he was unable to find anywhere to live in his adopted Florence, so he returned to his native Romagna and had chosen to make his home there in a remote valley, because it looked so pastoral and untouched by war. Indeed, there seemed no reason why it should ever be affected: but quite soon after he had settled in his new home, the Allies started to bomb the valley so regularly and to such an extent that it became known to the world as the Death Valley. He then moved to a hotel, and from hotel to hotel, till the end of the war. Some time during the years he had taken under his wing—if one can use the expression in this connection—a hen that he had found in the yard of a deserted and bombed farmhouse. She quickly became devoted to him and was widely known as La Gallina. She lived between his shirt and coat, buttoned in for security, and was the cause of most of his moves from hotel to hotel in the small cities of the region: for the other guests sitting in the public rooms of the establishment would object to the sudden contented sound of clucking and the emergence of a bright eye and the scruffy feathered neck above the lapel of Signor Bracciaforte's coat. The lounge, as the residents called it, was no place for fowls: she should never have been taken away from the farm. But he refused to abandon her and together they moved from place to place, from one hotel to another. Eventually, however, La Gallina died from old age, but tears still came into Signor Bracciaforte's eyes when he spoke of her. . . .

Signor Bracciaforte, I was explaining, was accompanying my father in his search for garden ornaments, as so often before on previous similar occasions, and leading the way, would turn to my father and say as he always did: 'Mebbee, we fine old t'ing.'

## THE FOUNTAIN

M Y FATHER was apt to drive too hard a bargain. . . . One morning in Treviso, whither he, with Signor Braccia-forte in attendance, had gone for the day from Venice, in the back garden of a dealer who lived on the ground floor of an old palace, and with whom they had transacted business on more than one occasion in the past—so that the *antiquario* must have grasped what technique would be used and what treatment to expect—my father at last discovered a fountain of the very size and shape he required. It was made of marble that when it had first been cut had been pure white, but now had assumed with the passing of time a tone of dark honey, and had been invested, further, with a perfect patina by centuries of exposure to salt air and to the lion-maned glare of the Venetian lagoons. It was plainly intended for him—indeed, the sole hindrance to its immediate purchase was the high price demanded by the dealer; too high even when my father had in his own mind deducted one third of the sum first asked, which constituted the

customary overcharge made by the vendor in order to allow
ample room for bargaining. Such was the common practice in
those days. Obviously the dealer enjoyed exercise in this
important art: he liked to bargain (in the manner, no doubt,
that a trout might enjoy being tickled). This my father
remembered from earlier visits to him.

In order to obtain the best results, my father, with Bracciaforte and Henry Moat in waiting, decided to move out to
Treviso for two weeks, during which period—fortunately the
hotel was situated near the apartment of the dealer—my
father could descend on him at any moment he chose of the
day or night. (The dealer, he averred, did not mind. It gave an
*antiquario* the feeling that he was doing his selfless duty—like
doctors whom 'we happen to know' nothing pleases more
than to be called up from their beds during the darkest and
most slumberous hours to attend an unknown patient with
little wrong with him. . . . But by this time the simile had
grown rather muddled and he abandoned it). . . . Treviso was a
pleasant place in which to make a stay and the hotel was a
singularly fine building, not very imaginative, he owned, but
built as if to battle against eternity single-handed; in fact it was
of a mysterious size and solidity, since few people would want
to stay there for long with Venice so near to entice them. There
did not seem to be even the usual solitary tourist looking as if
he had been pressed between the pages of a Baedeker. No, the
hotel was plainly empty and he and Signor Bracciaforte had
the undivided attention of the proprietor and staff.

The *antiquario* was a dapper little man with a charming
smile, albeit, after the first few mornings, afternoons, and
evenings of bargaining with my father that smile began to
crack, while by the last few days it had plainly gone rancid.
Nevertheless, he still retained at times an air of smiling to

himself at some joke which only himself could perceive.

My father conducted the proceedings with considerable skill: sudden bouts of bullying alternating with stretches of long but gentle persistence. By the ninth day the price had been brought to a reasonable level and by the thirteenth it became obvious that my father would get his way and that the next morning the *antiquario* was bound to accept the final offer, so that in the afternoon my father would be able to return to Venice floating in triumph from the station through the apotheositic splendours of a Venetian sunset to Danieli's Hotel.

Consequently, on the morning of the fourteenth day, and accompanied of course by Signor Bracciaforte, he arrived at the dealer's in a very genial humour, at an hour unusually early even for him, and ready to clinch his bargain. He rang the bell happily: but nobody answered. No doubt he had not pulled it hard enough. He rang again, more heavily: this time they both heard it ring. . . . Still no one came. Just as he was going to ring a third time, he happened to look down, and saw an envelope projecting from under the door. He picked it up. It was addressed to *Monsieur Sitwell*. He tore it open and read. . . . It began with many professions of esteem, and went on to say how much the dealer had enjoyed the sessions of bargaining at pleasantly unconventional hours, but now that he had sold this fountain at the same low price at which he had offered it to my father the previous afternoon, he felt the need of change and fresh air, and had decided on impulse to go to the country for a few days' shooting. . . . The purchaser of the fountain, as my father would undoubtedly know, was his compatriot, the Duke of Meldrum. . . . The Duke of Meldrum was reputed to be the richest man in England, with an income to spend—for this was before the introduction of surtax—of a thousand pounds a day. . . . My father was flabbergasted. He had not even been aware that the Duke was in the vicinity, far less that he was staying, as it transpired, at the same hotel; whereas the Duke had known that my father was there and bidding—one cannot say briskly, but seriously—and had arranged for the *antiquario* to telephone every evening to his courier, giving the score, as it were, of both parties at the close of play. Nor, even had my father known of the Duke being so near, would he have connected him with works of art: no, race-horses, polo, hunting, and yachts were his domain and speciality. My father was enraged. The more he thought about it, the more angry he became, as he dwelt in his mind on the hours he had wasted in unwitting preparations of a vicarious super-bargain for his invisible rival; in short, for having done all the work and got nothing for it.

If, during the years that immediately followed, a tourist were to obtain permission to visit Meldrum Abbey, after being taken to see the gold trophies won by the race-horses, which were displayed in a specially constructed chamber, a kind of strong-room cellar, and to marvel at the private post-office, police station, and dental surgery, he would then be sure to be conducted through the garden to admire the fountain, looking very out of keeping with grey skies in a damp yew-enclosed setting. By its side stood a wooden notice, painted green, with the following words inscribed on it in white letters:

This fountain, a gem of the Italian Renaissance, sculptured by the hand of Bartolomeo di Treviso, was discovered abroad by Henry Victor Fitzroy Fawcett, eleventh Duke of Meldrum, and erected by him in its present suitable position.

Further, to this very hour, when parties of tourists are shown round by the present Duke, a grandson, this cicerone will point out the fountain to his flocks and read aloud to them the legend.

[89]

## IDEAS FROM THE BUREAU

ONE morning not long ago I was sitting in the dentist's
chair when, just as he was walking away from it to
make sure what was happening in the next room from which
sounded a loud groaning, and leaving me with my mouth full
of looking-glasses, drills, steel crochet-hooks, and other
instruments of his profession, he remarked: 'I will say one
thing for you: you're a good listener.' At the time I was not
amused, but thinking it over I began to believe that there
might be a little truth in it, and that it was as the result of many
years of silent observation and suffering that I had become
something of an expert on parents and how to manage them.
Indeed, at one time in the twenties I had considered opening
an office where it would be possible to obtain professional
advice on payment of a fee. It was to be called *The Sons and
Daughters Advice Bureau* and would have existed in order to
advise children how to treat their parents, whether to try
temporarily to pacify or further to inflame them, always with

a view to subsequent relaxation. For this purpose, new techniques had to be devised.

Means of increasing nervous tension—in fact the waging of a private cold war—are not difficult to invent. . . . It was during the twenties, after my father had been vouchsafed the vision of the Phantom Tax-inspector and when, as a result, he was in a rather nervous condition, that I considered using on him one of the three techniques that I had devised for the harrying of Percy Wyndham Lewis, a person also of deeply suspicious nature. The first process is called *The Masked Musicians*, the second I named *The Unexpected Gift*, and the third *The Quick-change Artiste*.

At Renishaw one year I had spent a long, wet summer morning looking round a lumber-room—limbo-room would have been a more precise description of this place where the William Morris paper hung from the walls like the tattered regimental banners of a defeated foreign foe in a cathedral, and a piled-up clutter of unwanted objects led an existence in a half-world of dust: an old piano, a stuffed bird of dull but unknown species—a sort of seagull I suppose—a Venetian vase of blue-green glass over six foot in height and resembling in shape a trumpet only with a crinkled edge, a few assegais and a shield made from some kind of Zulu esparto grass, a carved, carpenter's-gothic armchair, a harp, a plumed hat in a case, belonging to an extinct uniform which had got itself elsewhere, a great many cut-glass scent-bottles with silver tops now black, bits of broken cups and saucers, a hare made of blue china with an eyeglass and high white collar, and a box of photographs all faded to the colour of khaki. Among these one caught my eye and filled me with curiosity. It showed two men sitting side by side, both dressed in the same way and looking exactly alike. They were wearing black felt hats drawn down over their eyes and enveloping black cloaks, very mysterious; but what captivated me was that they were both the very image of Wyndham Lewis. My mother was the only person who might be able to identify them. I went to find her. She looked at them and said:

'Of course, they are the Masked Musicians.'

This was tantalizing because she could tell me no more. The photograph must have been very nearly forty years old. . . . I acted at once and ordered five hundred picture postcards to be reproduced from it, and when they arrived I sent a large number of them to Wyndham Lewis's particular friends and particular enemies: but the first card of all I posted was addressed to Wyndham Lewis himself at his studio with written on it anonymously the intimidating message: 'So there *are* two of you!' . . .

Puzzled and alarmed, he went round to see various friends and found them with the same photograph, placed in a conspicuous position on the mantelpiece, but everyone was equally unable to explain the meaning.

I will now tell the reader how the idea of the second method came to me as the happy result of a fortunate concatenation of circumstances. . . . One morning I came downstairs and said to my secretary, who was always most co-operative: 'I feel just in the mood to send Wyndham Lewis an unsolicited gift. . . . I wonder what we could find for him today.'

She replied: 'I've the very thing for him in an envelope in my bag. It's a tooth, extracted by the dentist yesterday. . . . Here it is!' and she triumphantly produced on the palm of her hand an opalescent molar.

I at once accepted the kind offer: first I wrapped the precious object in cotton wool and next placed it in a cardboard box, which had contained a watch, was of a pale shade of lilac, and bore on the lid in gold lettering the famous name of Cartier. I then added a card that I found lying on my desk, and which bore engraved on it the legend: *With Sir Gerald du Maurier's Compliments.* (It must have reached me, I think, accompanying an appeal for some charity connected with the stage, and affords another instance of the folly of throwing anything away—you can never tell when the most improbable article may come in useful.) The whole surprise packet, after it had been wound in layer after layer of rustling tissue paper, was then encased in sober brown paper, on which was pasted securely a label bearing Wyndham Lewis's name and address in typescript. Finally, when all this had been accomplished, it was posted to him from the G.P.O. . . . . The essence of the Unsolicited Gift is the artful combination of unrelated objects. I tried to think of some equally exciting present for my father, but no inspiration came. . . . Perhaps the third technique I had invented, known as *The Quick-change Artiste,* could be more easily applied to parents.

There were turns—now I fear defunct—still lingering in the superb music-hall programmes of those days, announced as being performed by Professor So-and-So, 'the World-famous Quick-change Artiste'. Dapper and clean-shaven, a man would walk on to the stage, empty except for one piece of furniture, a cross between a desk and a table, and bow to the audience; when the applause had died down, he would explain that his first impersonation would be of Gounod. He would then turn his back on the auditorium and go to the table, as we will call it, where his fingers would move quickly among a collection of wigs, false noses, and looking-glasses; having transformed himself, he would whisk round to the audience, at the same time striking a supposedly characteristic attitude, such as, in this instance, holding a conductor's baton as if about

to launch on the world a new masterpiece. This portrayal
would be greeted with rapturous applause, though in spite of
the reception the artiste had won, he had not, I apprehend, the
slightest conception, any more than I had myself, of what the
composer had looked like in real life. When the clapping had
died down, the performer would announce his next impersonation, which was nearly sure to be of the Abbé Liszt, an item
that appeared in such turns, as did that of Gounod, to be almost
obligatory. . . . Indeed, the imitations given by quick-change
artistes were almost always the same, and it was difficult to
grasp what principle of selection governed their choice, except
that a lot of hair on head and face made the impersonation
easier. The repertory generally included, in addition to Gounod
and the Abbé, Charles Dickens and some of the following:
Zola, Mr Gladstone, Lord Tennyson, Bismarck, and, to finish
up with, W. G. Grace, wearing a round cricket cap and carrying a bat. (This last was a certain winner.) It will have been
noticed that those who were impersonated all belonged
roughly to the same period, then the recent past, and were
seldom earlier than the Emperor Napoleon the Third or later
than President Kruger (Oom Paul, always such a great target
for fish-heads when they were in supply). Most of these figures,
in short, belonged to the limbo of those who had died some
thirty years before, and though in life they may have looked
immensely distinguished, the mimicry of them seemed now to
bring with it a whiff of Madame Tussaud's Chamber of Horrors,
and to declare their relationship to the wax effigies of Doctor
Neil Cream or of Charley Peace—who, we may recollect, was
himself a quick-change artiste, adept at totally changing his
appearance, even the lines of his face, in the shortest possible
time.

It will be appreciated that my father would have been

astonished if his eyes, wandering from the Phantom Tax-inspector on the roof of the next-door house down to the drive, had suddenly beheld there the apparition of Gounod, and hurrying into the house to fetch Robins or Henry to look at the startling new arrival, had returned in the space of two minutes only to find in his place Mr Gladstone or the Abbé Liszt. The prospect of his reactions would be fascinating—so alluring, indeed, that it was difficult to banish the idea: but there proved to be too many practical difficulties to its fruition. Quick-change artistes had already become very rare and those who still existed were old, and age has little liking for adventure, as we are frequently informed, so that the idea of hanging about all day under the damp shelter of umbrageous trees, and then meeting with an uncertain reception at the end of it, did not appeal to them. Moreover, if they agreed to perform for a day, they must be paid, they insisted, for a full week's engagement. . . . We had therefore to remain content with the Phantom Tax-inspector.

# 13

## LOOKING AHEAD

ONE morning in the hot summer of 1921 I was walking
with my father in the park at Renishaw, where great
patches of shadow lay under the old trees and at the edges of
the plantations. He was wearing a very neat, pale grey suit and
a grey wide-awake hat. As we were approaching a fence with
a wooden gate, he suddenly took a little run and vaulted lightly
over it. I was astonished, for he was over sixty years of age,
complained always that the slightest exertion tired him out,
and, additional cause for wonder, I had never seen him do this
before. He must have noticed my surprise, for he said to me: 'I
try to keep up my vaulting, to amuse my friends.' My father,
though he never saw any member of the spectral band,
continued often to allude to it.

My father always liked to pose to himself as a fine sports-
man, and the exploit I have just related helped to foster this
illusion. Certainly I can never recollect his hunting or riding
for pleasure—albeit I remember my mother telling me that he

Author's bedroom with Staffordshire Figures

Author standing by the Gothick Temple, Renishaw

had as a young man won a point-to-point; a victory the status
of which she somewhat disparaged by alleging that his horse
had run away with him. Nevertheless it brought him in some
votes at the subsequent Election, though of course it may have
cost him others. My mother also recalled how my grandmother
Sitwell, who disapproved of any form of racing because of the
opportunity it afforded for gambling, had remained in her
room in prayer, not for the victory of her son, but for his
safety, and how when eventually she rose from her knees,
and went downstairs and heard the result, she felt that such an
answer to her supplications had been almost overwhelmingly
too swift, direct, and triumphant: so she climbed upstairs again,
and spent the rest of the day imploring the Deity to turn
a disapproving eye on any further racing exploits of my
father's.

My father also objected strongly to gambling—and with
every reason—because his family had twice been ruined by
addiction to it—objected to it, that is to say, except on the
Stock Exchange, where it was promoted and given a new
name, being transformed into investment, that pillar of Church
and State, and at the worst being dignified by the word
*speculation*. Notwithstanding his principles, he liked to stay in
the metropolis of the gambling world, Monte Carlo. He never
entered the Rooms (a paternal deprivation which, indeed, I
welcomed, since it meant that I could frequent them with the
certainty of not meeting him), nor could he enjoy walking
through the acres of garden, of which he deplored the lay-out
('Such a pity not to have consulted *me*') as much as the floral
extravagance of the subtropical blossoms that flourished therein
in certain parts, plants such as the hibiscus with its red trumpet.
The tidiness of the ordinary Riviera flowers offended him
equally, beds of carnations, for instance, covered with sacking

every night during the winter months for protection against possible cold air. In short, he could take no pleasure in any of the flowers set in emeraldine grass with not a blade awry. So neat was everything that it seemed that the only explanation could be that every blade and blossom must have its own attendant. No, what he enjoyed, what drew him here, was the sense of lavishness which made the visitor realize that more money was spent on him than it cost him (so long as he did not go into the Rooms), that his stay was subsidized indirectly by the losses at the tables incurred by gamblers of many nations, and all these amenities just described, together with many others, were provided for him gratis through the errors and cupidity of people more foolish than himself. Moreover, all empty pockets were in his view deserved, for he would not allow the existence of good or bad fortune. In support, he would quote a favourite dictum: 'There is no such thing as good or bad luck, only good or bad management.' There were, of course, other drawbacks besides those enumerated which also prevented complete contentment. Thus in spite of his liking for the principality, he took exception to the architectural style of the Casino and its immediate neighbours, and I recall his remarking to me at tea one afternoon in the Café de Paris:

'Have you noticed that the buildings here have a most objectionable gaiety about them?'

It was during the visit to my father at Monte Carlo that he issued the wildest and most terrifying of all his warnings to me. Readers of those books of mine in which my father occurs may remember that he was wont to give strange cautions to those round him. As he grew older these seemed to become more unexpected and frequent. We had been talking the previous evening of my projected first visit to the United States early in the New Year. In the morning he sent for me to his room. As I entered, he said: 'Good morning, Osbert, come in and shut the door. . . . There are two things of which I should warn you before you start for America.'

My heart sank at the familiar opening, usually the preliminary to trouble.

'What are they, Father?'

'Never play with a dead cat, and above all never make friends with a monkey.'

Even I, accustomed though I was to receiving from him cautions at once morbid and startling, was on this occasion somewhat disconcerted, because the warnings thus addressed to me seemed to fit in with no proclivities of my nature of which I was conscious. Good heavens, what could he mean? Indeed, I was so much taken aback that I rather foolishly asked: 'Why?', and received a yet more bewildering Delphic reply delivered in his most withering style:

'Because if you do you'll get diphtheria!'

The explanation proved to be that my father had read in one of the papers of an outbreak in New York of this illness, which a small boy had developed; and the child had been seen playing in Central Park, throwing the body of a dead cat up in the air and catching it over and over again. The second warning derived also from a newspaper, in the columns of which he had read how some children had been observed, pressed against the bars of a cage in the Zoo, talking for a long time to a great ape, and that in view of the fact that the animal had developed diphtheria the next day, it was surmised in medical circles that the children, who fell ill a week or two later, had contracted the disease from their anthropoid chum. (My father was fond of animals, and I have often seen him go up to the cage of a monkey, and talk to the sad-eyed but

[99]

insouciant inmate. . . . His special interest in the simian tribes was no doubt a tribute to the part they played in the evolutionary theories of his great hero Charles Darwin.) That, however, which rendered my father's warnings disturbing as well as entertaining was that you could not just dismiss them, because you never knew what might not come next, and because often under their *prima facie* absurdity would lurk, hidden by piles of rubbish though it might be, an unexpected truth. Equally, his mind, with its conflicting streaks of conventional and unconventional, on occasions enabled him to arrive at startling but perhaps correct conclusions—as, for example, when we entered into argument about a contemporary trial for murder; in the course of our dispute I opined that the man found guilty was plainly a lunatic and should, therefore, not be executed: my father agreed, rather surprisingly, that the man was mad, but added: 'and one of his delusions may be that he can always commit a murder with absolute impunity'.

My father had a great belief in 'Looking Ahead', which had become with him a special process and one which was concerned with material affairs and not, as might have been presumed from its name, with some spiritual state in the future. No, 'Looking Ahead' was included in good management and was avoided whenever possible by my mother. The concentration necessary to its formulation sometimes gave 'Looking Ahead' an impression of insensibility which was not altogether deserved. It had to be impersonal as a proposition in geometry, and who has ever complained that Euclid was heartless? . . . My mother related to me one of the most singular instances of it. The scene had taken place in March 1916, while I was in the trenches. My father had one morning rushed like a whirlwind into the room, and said at great speed: 'I have just been looking ahead. We may hear at any moment that Osbert's been killed, and the other dear boy will probably go too; in which case you will certainly pass away, and what I want to know is, would the money in your settlement be available for the sons of my second marriage?'

## 14

## UNFORGOTTEN FEASTS

PROVERBS are often supposed to embalm and preserve an ancient truth: nevertheless, to the precise contrary, they may on occasion present in its stead a stunning falsity. Thus, enough is *not* as good as a feast and never will be. An adequacy may be honest and healthy but lacks the glamour of a feast. The idea of the banquets given by the City Companies fascinated me as a small boy and conferred upon my father a special prestige in my eyes, because he would from time to time go up to London in order to attend a gala of this kind, and return the next day bringing with him an elaborate box of chocolates or some piece of glass or china which had been given to him as a memento. Ordinarily, however, banquets and feasts bore no part in my father's life, though he took an interest in the decorative and esthetic side of them and would sometimes talk with apparent airy approval of the singular entertainments offered in Rome by that Syrian esthete, the teen-age Emperor Heliogabalus, some two thousand years before. No! A nourishing and unexciting sufficiency was as a rule the culinary standard my father supported. He liked food to be tasteless and to be served tepid: though he had a good appetite and ate very quickly—a habit which he was fond of attributing to the rapidity of the working of his brain. His favourite dish was blancmange, that quaking white confection that masquerades under a bogus foreign title but is quite unknown in the whole gastronomic repertory of the French. So fond was he of it, and so often did it figure in the menu, that Henry would warn us beforehand: 'He's having his old rock of ages again for luncheon.' It will be understood that for a good cook to have to send up that concoction would be derogatory; and how often have I not heard my mother declare that he could ruin the best chef in the world, if left alone with him for two days to order and superintend the meals. The poor cook would hereafter abide in a fog of frustrated virtuosity. Yet though my father in no whit resembled or aspired to resemble either Lucullus as gourmet or Trimalchio as host, nevertheless at least two of the dinner-parties he gave in his later years at Montegufoni attained a certain more than local celebrity.

While the first dinner-party described pertained to the ancient and international world of slap-stick, it is really with the second and in essence fantastic and mysterious occasion that I am chiefly concerned. It was essentially of a socialitic nature. The guests were comparatively few and chosen on no very evident principle. For that reason it is necessary to consider and describe two of the persons present, but although they occur in the second part of this chapter, I present them here so as not to allow the description of the persons to interfere with the detailing of the two parties placed together for comparison.

First, Mrs George Keppel: a most unusual person who

naturally dominated, but never domineered over, the people in her company. To such a degree was this the case that I may add that when in 1940 at the end of the phoney war I stayed at Monte Carlo on my way back from Italy about ten days before the occupation of Paris by the Germans and just before Italy joined in the war, I saw in the dining-room of the Hôtel de Paris several of those who frequented the same circles as she did; when they in turn beckoned to me, the question they asked was identical. It was not, as I had rather expected: 'Is Italy coming into the war?' but instead: 'Is Alice Keppel still in Florence?' . . . She was not a beautiful woman, but had a handsome and very individual appearance. In addition, she was, to use a colloquialism of her time, 'great fun'. Jewels suited her and there was about her a certain natural magnificence which was always reflected in her surroundings. Thus her villa in Florence had the same splendour about it that her house in Grosvenor Street had formerly shown. . . . She added an ambience of amusement, good nature, and keen appreciation both of the surface and of what was occurring underneath it to any occasion at which she was present. As she talked in her clear and level voice, her bold and humorous grey-green eyes raked the scene and took in all that was happening. To give an example of her particular quality, I recall an incident that took place a year or two earlier at Renishaw when she was staying with us. A man whom we had never seen before was wished on us for luncheon one day. He was placed next to my sister, and took it into his head to enquire of her: 'Do you remember this house being built, Miss Sitwell?' Mrs Keppel overheard this, and said to him quickly: 'My dear man, be careful! Not even the nicest girl in the world likes to be asked if she is four hundred years old.'

Then, my aunt Londesborough: she was by now an old

lady. Without being fat, she gave the impression of being over
life-size, and when she walked into a room, with a slight limp
that was the result of a fall out hunting, she certainly looked an
imposing figure, an Amazonian wreck, a substantial ruin of the
Edwardian Age of which—in every sense of the word—she
had been a prop. . . . My father did not share my views of her
personal appearance, and when I one day asked him how my
aunt had looked as a girl, he had replied: 'Just as she does now
—always very flashy-looking'! But then he was prejudiced.
He had never forgiven her for having bought at a local
Conservative Bazaar a stone garden seat, somewhat fancifully
classified as Italian, but whatever its origin may have been, of
a quite unusual ugliness and an excruciating discomfort, and
then, having declared in public that she had purchased it as
a present for her brother-in-law, for having sent him in a bill
of fourteen pounds for it—after which there was yet more
talk than customarily of its being 'easy to be generous with
other people's money'. Even now, after the passage of many
years, the gift had been neither forgiven nor forgotten. Of
course it may be that the bill was an error due to her absent-
mindedness. She was, as will be seen, very vague. . . .

Here I produce in evidence a scrap of conversation I heard
at dinner one night during this same visit to Montegufoni; a
fragment typical of both participants.

'George,' my aunt said, 'on my way home I'd like to stay at
Monte Carlo—if only I knew where it was.'

My father, always delighted at the thought of perhaps being
able to stop anyone from doing something pleasurable, at any
rate in prospect, and as if he could detect some terrible danger
lurking and looming, at once replied:

'Oh, I shouldn't do anything as rash as that if I were you.'

I recalled, as I looked at her, how a cousin of mine had told me that at the Coronation of King Edward the Seventh, instructions having been specially issued by the Earl Marshal that peeresses were not to wear flowers, a distracted court official had rushed up to my cousin and wailed: 'What *am* I to do? Lady Londesborough has entered the Abbey wearing a large bouquet of pink malmaisons on her chest!' 'What are you to do?' my cousin replied. 'Go back to the Abbey and thank God that she isn't wearing them in her hair!' . . .

In her talk my aunt combined a singular eighteenth-century frankness with a degree of nineteenth-century squeamishness as well. To illustrate this trait, Henry Moat alleged that when, during this visit to Montegufoni, he went upstairs, he would often meet my aunt passing by in a dressing-gown, and each time it had occurred, feeling that some explanation was due from her, he asserted that she would invariably remark:

'I am just on my way to wash my feet.'

## THE NIGHT OF THE PARTY

### I

The International Festival of Modern Music, under the chairmanship of our old friend Edward Dent, was holding its annual festival at Siena in September 1929. This was for him a fortunate choice because Dent was never happier than when in Italy, and—which constituted an astonishing achievement for an Englishman—or, as for that, for an Italian—he could speak perfectly the dialect of every district and former sovereign state. For the festival the ancient city was crammed for ten days with visitors of a different kind from the ordinary tourist:

with those who brought to music a modern ear. . . . There was a house-party for the occasion at Montegufoni, because among works to be presented was *Façade*, and the author, the composer, and the reciter—my sister, William Walton, and Constant Lambert—were all three staying with us, and were eager to observe the impact of this entertainment upon the two worlds that would form its audience: the cosmopolitan, including advanced composers from nearly every civilized country, superimposed upon the lively Italian main body of it. In addition to the concert, a very full programme of festivities included a special performance of the *Palio*, that great Sienese spectacle, which had been arranged in honour of the visitors. (I recall that just before the *Palio* was due to start, William and Constant, plainly after a very good luncheon, walked with dignity, though with a slight but telling lurch, across the Piazza del Campo, the centre of which had now been cleared for the imminent horse-race, and that their stately intrepidity won them a resounding cheer from the great crowds pressed but jostling behind the barriers.) Though every day was crammed, there was a free evening at the end of the last concert, and accordingly we determined to try to induce my father to invite the delegates to dinner. We cherished little hope of success, but to our surprise he proved on this occasion to be malleable, and even eager to fall in with our plan.

Invitations were sent out and accepted; and on the last day of the festival, dinner was laid for seventy-two persons in the Great Dining-Room. The room had certainly not been used for a century and a half for this, its appointed purpose, and my father's choice of it on this occasion no doubt explained why he had allowed himself to be so easily persuaded; because he had lately restored it, made a kitchen underneath, and had installed as well a service lift to communicate with it. Now he wanted to see the room in action. It is nearly sixty feet long, and has a high coved ceiling, in the centre of which is shown, in a framing of decorative white stucco, an attractive piece of colour, a painted apotheosis, not so much of Cardinal Acciaiuoli, as of his hat, which is being conveyed up to heaven in a swirl of fleecy clouds and angels. On the north side five windows look toward Mont' Albano—in a village at the foot of which Leonardo da Vinci was born—and to the south, on to the Great Court. Between the windows are seventeenth-century plaster pedestal-brackets culminating in bat-like faces which in their deliberate distortion rival gothic gargoyles. My father as he hurried past them was wont to murmur: '*Brutto Seicento!*', but they must have nobly fulfilled their evident purpose: to support baroque dynastic busts which had long vanished, for all the pomp and pride of their full-bottomed wigs and Habsburg features.

Dinner was to be at quarter to seven, and the first guests, headed by Edward Dent, arrived at four-thirty, in order to help in welcoming the delegates unknown to us: the main body was to make the journey in two specially chartered charabancs, due to appear at six. Unfortunately, someone—and I can guess who it was, an indefatigable, indeed relentless, sightseer—had advised the organizers to pay a visit first to San Gimignano, and then to Volterra, so that the parties could see these ancient cities. It would take no time, he had said, as they were practically on the way. . . . But that afternoon they seemed a long distance out of it. The drivers of the charabancs continually lost their bearings, and wandered hither and thither for hours over Tuscany in the gloaming. Meanwhile my father stood in the Court of the Dukes of Athens, watch in hand, and would not be comforted. The waiters, hired for the occasion from Doney's in Florence, tall, melancholy, distinguished-looking individuals, immaculately tailored, spent the spare hours in musing or in throwing the stones with which we provided them down the Well of Polidora in the Great Court and, as its full depth was revealed to them by the sound and sight of the falling pebbles, they would exclaim in tones of astonished pleasure: '*Mamma Mia! Mamma Mia!*': but darkness soon crept over the world and we had to substitute burning straw for pebbles.

Electric light had not yet been installed, and although candles and lamps were provided in great quantities, the enormous blackness within the Castle seemed to swallow and suffocate such light as there was. Gloom brooded and doubts began to develop as to whether our expected guests would ever make their appearance. The principals were at a loss to explain the breakdown of the programme, and my father was full of reproaches, spoken and unspoken, and worked himself up into almost a fever of fussing. In fact he began to 'create'. What could have occurred? Motor-coaches were always dangerous. Perhaps they had fallen over a precipice—a dreadful thing to happen—or one of the drivers might have had a stroke at the wheel, or perhaps he had run amok—driving, he had always understood, could impose a great strain on a man—or, worse still, had the two charabancs through some mischance telescoped each other?—or—but here another side of the matter struck him: if there were no explanation of the sort he had outlined, it was grossly inconsiderate of the delegates. It was now long past the hour for dinner. . . . The sole consolation in our present quandary was that Henry Moat had entered my father's service once again, and though he was by now physically very heavy, lightness had returned to the air, and it was amusing to see how quickly he and my father took up their accustomed roles opposite each other. On this occasion my father called to him.

'Henry, it is now eight-thirty: if they don't arrive in ten minutes' time, I intend to sit down to dinner—if necessary by myself.'

'Well, Sir George, you couldn't ask for more cheerful company, could you?'

My father was just going to reply to this double-edged compliment when at that very moment an excited clamour composed of the shouts, shrieks, and lamentations of a furious mob could be heard approaching; it was the first contingent of guests. Distracted by the nightmare journey to which they had been subjected, always, it seemed to them, brought up with a sudden creaking of overstrained brakes on the very edge of an abyss, lost on mountain roads and in forests of total blackness—difficult enough to find your way about in even by daylight—now maddened by hunger and thirst and other natural needs of the human body, in their search for comfort the herd broke loose and charged about in the vast interior darkness of the Castle. The members of our house-party tried to help them, but they would not be guided; as they dashed down passages, they engaged in personal combat with inanimate objects, hitting here the corner of a cupboard, receiving there a black eye from a toppling *torciere*, were tripped by a lurking footstool, had a K.O. administered to them by an invisible table, or were victims of some infamous attack by a carved saint, who had apparently become an adept at all-in wrestling. Suddenly the vociferation, bawling, and trampling were redoubled; the second charabanc had at last made its appearance. Mob fought mob. Pandemonium reigned. The scene, as occasionally a lamp or candle revealed this conflict of shadows, was memorable, and in spite of the international composition of the mob, it was plain that only an English artist, Rowlandson, could have faithfully recorded the riot.

[110]

Eventually, however, the guests were rounded up and the mob began to break down into individuals again, as they were conducted to the places reserved for them in the Great Dining-Room, where we found friends and acquaintances—among them Edwin Evans and Spike Hughes—already in their chairs. We sat down exactly three hours late, but miraculously the food was not spoilt. . . . The waiters had recovered their official mien, and Henry Moat could be seen growing more portly and more dignified with every passing moment. Upstairs and downstairs wine flowed like—I was going to write 'like water', but in Tuscany water only flows in fountains—no, flowed like *wine*. When dinner was over, and the ladies retired, several of the male guests—especially those from Balkan countries—instead of standing up, fell down.

No one was tempted to stop and sightsee on the way home, for even this simple return journey to Siena in the dark would take two hours. At the Castle silence once more clothed the walls, though the sense of mystery was a little dispelled by the commonsense croaking of mud-happy frogs.

## THE NIGHT OF THE PARTY[1]

### II

The dinner-party to which we must now direct our attention took place in 1930; in early May, when the wistaria is in flower uncontaminated as yet by rain and distils its perfume far and

[1] I am grateful to Mrs Sacheverell Sitwell and to Mr David Horner for the help they have given me. . . . There were present, as well, Lady Londesborough and Lord Berners, who were both staying in the house, Mrs George Keppel who brought over from her villa at Bellosguardo her two daughters Violet and Sonia and her brother-in-law Lord Albemarle with his son Lord Bury and his daughter, and Sir John Aird.

wide, when the banksia roses cascade over the high walls of
the terraces and in the evening love-hungry female fire-flies
signal their presence to the more reticent males, and points of
light wax and wane and flicker through the warm and fragrant
darkness. . . . My sister-in-law Georgia and my brother and
David Horner and myself had been on a tour in Greece. We
stopped in Rome on our way to Montegufoni, where we had
been commanded to stay without fail during the last days of
April, but when we reached our hotel we found letters
waiting for us from my father. He asked Georgia to go there
three days earlier for some mysterious reason which he did not
divulge, and requested the rest of the party to delay their
arrival for a few days. Berners, who was going with us, suggested that we should spend three or four nights at Assisi. (I
shall always remember the first dinner there. . . . The dining-
room was full of mute esthetes and pallid ascetics whispering
over their meal and half a bottle of white wine—when suddenly
shock-treatment was administered by Sir John Squire, who—
we did not know he was in Assisi; neither, I think, did he—
burst through the door and shouted at us: 'Have you any
whisky in your pub? Mine has completely run out.' As a result
guests at the other tables fell silent and then began to talk in
ordinary tones.) It was during this visit to Assisi that I heard of
the death, following a sudden operation for appendicitis, of
Mrs Powell, my dear housekeeper in London, which greatly
saddened me and made me feel unusually impatient with what
was about to take place.

Later Georgia described to me her reception. . . . On
arrival, the motor—the Ark, which the readers of *Laughter in
the Next Room* may remember—had met her at the station.
Even the conniving manner of the driver seemed to suggest a
share in some mystification. . . . My mother was in one of her

[112]

rages, due to the fact that she could tell that some arcane matter was in the air and that my father was evidently planning something big but was determined not to let her into the secret. On the other hand, directly Georgia set foot in the precincts of the Castle my father, adopting a most confidential mien, dragged her off to talk in a distant room, thereby increasing my mother's anger. Our aunt Londesborough, the only other guest who had appeared as yet, vainly and ineptly tried to keep the peace between my parents, but the effort remained unsuccessful. To Georgia, though my father gave the impression that he was going to tell her of his schemes, he refused to reveal at present what he was planning, but his aim was plain: to work her up to a state of excitement rivalling his own. . . . Next morning he sent for her again, and again gave her noncohering pieces of information. But at last he made clear what he wanted from her: her help in making the whole of the plans as dramatic as possible. For the remaining days before the party he would dash into the gallery beckoning wildly to Georgia; thus continuing further to inflame my mother's mood. On Tuesday my sister-in-law had been obliged to start for Florence with my father at eight o'clock in the morning in order to complete arrangements for the all-important Thursday evening. When they returned, he immediately kidnapped her again, still without revealing the entire plans. Her diary for the day contains the entry 'sinister, eccentric, delirious'; no doubt an accurate summing up of the atmosphere.

The next day Georgia was to dine at the Keppels' villa, but in the morning came the not infrequent announcement that the Ark had broken down. The prospect seemed hopeless, as there was no means of letting her hostess know. However, Mrs Keppel discovered somehow or other and rescued her. . . . When she reached the villa she found a large party, members of which besieged her with questions about what was to happen the following evening. They were all aware that some mystery brooded. Her position was more especially difficult because my father had at last revealed to her the full plans, first having sworn her to an embarrassing secrecy; which, the next day, was to make her relations with my mother still more unenviable.

My mother, dressed in black, spent the day in her favourite armchair by an open french window, and with numberless copies of English newspapers drifting round her feet, as if deposited there by a receding tide. Occasionally she would lunge ineffectually with a fly-whisk at some large velvety insect that steered itself in on a puff of golden fragrance from the garden, or would remark to someone passing through the gallery: 'All one can do is to live from day to day.'

I remember that in the afternoon my father passed rapidly by her in the Cardinal's Garden, and she called out: 'George, you're looking just like Bobby Arthington'—a cousin of his for whom she entertained no admiration, so that the alleged resemblance was certainly not intended as a compliment. My father, however, treated it as such, fluttered his hand at her and with a radiant air called back: 'So glad!'

However, in any case, my mother took a dejected view of the party. Her own contribution to the evening had been to order two dozen bottles of champagne, but my father, who had only found out about them when the cases were at the door, refused to accept delivery, explaining to my mother that the red wine of the Castle would be much more appreciated by the guests. My mother said:

'But, George, champagne makes everyone feel so cheerful.'

'But I'm not sure that I *want* them to feel *cheerful*. It isn't the mood I'm aiming at.'

This reply must have related to the special character of the

[114]

party which was to take place—as no doubt did the fact that the dinner was laid in the Grand Sala, a large very high room across the Great Court opposite that room in which the dinner already described had taken place.

On arrival at Montegufoni it was plain that some mystery was hatching, but nobody seemed to know what or why. Henry refused to enlighten us—if, indeed, he were in the secret. . . . A volcanic air permeated everything and everyone seemed in bad humour. From the symptoms I could not diagnose the illness, though I ought from previous experience to have been able to deduce what sort of business was brewing; it was presumably one of those dim, demi-practical jokes to which my father was partial; as for example when he brought out on the 1st January 1901 a prophetic issue of the *Scarborough Post* (a local paper which for many years belonged to him), dated 1st January 2001—one of those jokes the fun of which resided more in the months of preparation they required beforehand than in the whimper and splutter of the resulting finale.

Georgia could not, or rather would not, enlighten us.

.        .        .        .

The Sala commanded the sharp declivities of the garden; the walls, slanting back at the angle only to be found in walls built in Rome and Tuscany, and seeming to bring a remote echo of temple terraces in Cambodia, were hidden now under the clustered knots and buds of the climbing roses, and revealed the wide expanse of country beyond the cypress groves and spring woods and the fields redolent of flowering bean. On the west was a door which disclosed, when open, a vista of painted rooms. . . . A meal in the Grand Sala was in itself an innovation, and therefore probably the choice of it must be connected with the nature of the mystery, but I held no clue.

My father sat at the head of a long table, looking imperturbably good-humoured, by no means a true or at any rate an abiding aspect of his character. He also had somewhat the air of a conjurer about to produce a rabbit from his hat. Occasionally he would look round in a rapt manner, which I took to signify that he was thinking of early times when the Duke of Athens used to come here attended by five hundred Greeklings to visit his brother.

Dinner had started and continued in an ordinary enough way until the last course was handed round, when Angelo the *contadino* came in and whispered something to my father, who got up, saying: 'Somebody wants to speak to me', and hurried away, returning in about five minutes. He then said to Mrs Keppel, who was sitting on his right: 'The workmen have found a ghost: will you come and inspect it with me?' . . . When they came back he went up to someone else, and said the same thing, repeating the formula to each guest in turn. . . . The guests came back looking startled and bewildered. My aunt Londesborough looked frightened. Sachie was worried and distraught. 'It's simply Bouvard and Pécuchet,' he complained, 'and makes us all look such fools.' I remember one old gentleman saying to me over and over again: 'But what does it *mean*? I can't make head or tail of it!'

I could not enlighten him, since I had not yet been conducted, but at last my turn came. I did not want to go, for I am not by nature very inquisitive: moreover I thought it just possible that a ghost *had* been found. Nevertheless, since the visit was clearly obligatory, I went. My father led me through the painted apartments, to the end of the Galleria, the principal drawing-room, then he opened a door, which could not be

seen unless you knew of it, and took me down a few break-
neck stairs and through a crack-skull door into another room
of the very existence of which we had been unaware: in the far
wall a large jagged hole had been knocked, and through it could
be seen a further secret chamber. In the foreground stood a
table at which sat a middle-aged man with a sallow face, dressed
in the scarlet robes of a Cardinal. On the table lay a vellum-
coloured holy book of some sort, and a human skull. The
Cardinal was repeating over and over again with a strong
cockney accent: 'Perchè non mi lasciano in pace?' I soon recog-
nized him as an Englishman, an habitual of the Castle.

The room was lofty for its size, and behind the figure stood,
fixed to the wall, a series of gothic cupboards, in cypress wood,
with elaborately carved borders to the larger panels and with a
fretwork cornice. The table, a rare example of its kind,
belonged to the earliest days of Italian furniture.

By the time we had returned to the dinner table we found
an atmosphere of bewilderment amounting almost to stupe-
faction brooding over the guests. (This was, I think, the mood
at which my father was aiming; he may not have wished his
guests to feel cheerful, but he *did* want them to feel astonished,
even flabbergasted.) The same old gentleman as before was
still loud in his demand for help in understanding what was
taking place. 'What is the old fellow supposed to *be*?' he
repeated. '*Someone must know.*' But nobody could or would
enlighten him. Looking back, I suppose the correct answer
would have been: 'One of the two Cardinals produced by
the Acciaiuoli family.' . . . But though the reply would
have sounded so indefinite, even then the dates would not
tally. . . . I should have told him that my father had designed
the whole occasion as an attempt, as so often before,
'to amuse my friends', that phantom company to whose

existence he so often and loyally referred. I ought to have added that 'amuse my friends' was a common phrase with my father, and that the fun in this instance resided in the fact that, except for himself and Georgia, no one present, my mother included, had been aware of the existence of the room disclosed this evening, that it must have taken months to prepare, workmen labouring at it day after day, always from the other side of the wall, and that they had only broken through it during the time occupied by the first few courses at dinner. I ought, too, to have explained to him that the bookshelves, so-called, had been copied in detail from a cupboard in a picture by Carpaccio—and in this connection I should have indicated to him what I have, I hope, elsewhere made clear to my readers, that in this characteristic we reach an instance of one of my father's special mental attitudes. At first anyone acquainted with him would have presumed, because of his general esthetic outlook, that he was interested in early Italian painting because of its beauty: but this would have been a false deduction; no, he only took notice of any particular painting if it contained some object, spoon or fork for example, or, as in this instance, a cupboard, that would be suitable for him to reproduce at Montegufoni (at the restoration of which he had now been at work for at least twenty years without apparently coming any nearer the end of it); otherwise he would give a picture only a cursory glance, and hurry on, saying: 'It has nothing in it for me!' as if pictures had been painted with only that sole prophetic aim in view, and if they failed in this respect were a complete waste of time and effort. When, on the other hand, he succeeded in finding some detail that might be suitable, he would stand in front of the picture for an unconscionable time, gazing at it intently, and would then scribble some notes with a stub of a pencil on the back of an old envelope which he carried about with him in his pocket for that purpose, and perhaps he would also add a little rough drawing—but now we must return to the party.

Everybody appeared to be embarrassed, but I was told that my aunt Londesborough had kept her head and had attempted an explanation to her escort, remarking: 'It must be a sort of tomb, I think. I can't hear what he's saying. He must be a Cardinal . . . or one of those what-d'you-callums . . . you know, dear boy.'

In any case, however, though she had made the best of it, this cannot have been her idea of a party. Skulls and hermits were not in her line: no, for her the word *party* summoned up the memory of great entertainments given at St Dunstan's for King Edward and Queen Alexandra, the gardens illuminated, the rooms crammed with malmaisons and roses, and quails and champagne, and, behind her, her Indian page in pink clothes with a pink turban.

Soon the questionings of his guests were drowned by the clamour and clatter of the brass band of *La Società Filarmònica di Montegufoni* which started to play outside in the court. Their programme began with a village version of 'God Save the King', with many idiosyncratic variations: these lasted for half an hour, during which time we had all to stand to attention in the court facing the bandsmen. As the piece at last began to show signs of abating, my aunt, who stood beside me, said in my ear:

'Osbert, you were in the Brigade of Guards. Stand in front of Alice Keppel immediately! Otherwise she'll take the salute.' I looked round, and there, sure enough, was Mrs Keppel preparing to charge through the vanguard.

After the National Anthem had finished we danced in the court to the strains of lively, outmoded waltzes, grown rustic by the passage of time. It was a hot night and my aunt Londes-

[119]

borough and her partner had found seats in a window. The conversation went somewhat as follows:

'I've bought a new house called Mill Hill Lodge,' she observed.

'Where is it?'

'I'm not quite sure *where*, but it's on Barnes Common, wherever that is. There are two roads to London; which make it very convenient in a fog.'

I then came up to ask my aunt to dance. We glided off rather stiffly. She returned out of breath, but elated by the waltz. 'I know what,' she exclaimed, 'I'll give a ball at Mill Hill Lodge when I get back! Electric lights—coloured ones—in the garden in the trees, and *you* will choose the band, but we must have plenty of valses, dear boy. But of course there are those couples on Barnes Common . . . they lie there, you know.'

Time passed, and our guests departed into the darkness, which, on the point of 'What is it all about?', matched this incident; but the darkness was thronged with dancing dots of light, supplied by the fire-flies, and fragrant with the scent of honeysuckle. Most of the guests were still in a daze, but, to this day, if they meet, the survivors still discuss the party and the memory of it forms a link between them.

The following morning an edict was issued that the newly discovered room would be known in future as the Gothic Library. For a time it served a purpose; whenever anything particularly absurd happened it was possible to go there quietly and laugh it out—such an incident had occurred the following evening when my aunt Londesborough decided to read aloud the current *Fragrant Minute* by Wilhelmina Stitch from the latest copy of the *Daily Sketch*. . . . It also at moments served the purpose of supplying a solemn background for family announcements, as the reader will see in another chapter 'Making a Bolt for It'. . . . During the war the Castle was occupied in turn by the troops of many nations. The Fortuny curtains of the Gothic Library were subsequently used by the German soldiers to clean their boots. The smooth, vellum-coloured walls still palely retain on them, drawn in chalk, the regimental emblems of victorious South African and New Zealand regiments.

## 15

## BY RAIL AND BOAT

TRAVELLING by rail with my father and mother always presented its own tortures as well as its own pleasures. What vistas of journeys with one or other or both my memory treasures and re-creates; journeys from Scarborough to London, for instance, in an extinct kind of railway carriage called a saloon, rather resembling, only of course much smaller than, a private Pullman car. It had wide windows and on the ceiling a gas jet blossomed like an evening primrose under its thick bell-glass. It also contained a table on which to place the luncheon baskets, made of polished and creaking brown wicker, which we would invariably buy at York station. There we would stop just long enough to take them on board and to be formally greeted by one of Henry Moat's elder brothers who was for many years stationmaster and, when on duty, always wore a top hat and frock-coat as became his dignity. Then we would be shunted to join the London train. The luncheon, when taken out of the baskets with a great rustling and crackling of grease-proof paper—and after we had survived the recurrent disappointment caused by unwrapping layer after layer from one large packet to find it consisted only of a particle of salt—always in the end revealed cold chicken, cooked long ago, or, it may be, smoked by the engines that snorted their funnels off in York station. These chickens posed as well an educational puzzle: were they claiming to have been educated at Eton or at Harrow, because, though they had plainly been the right age to enter—or, as for that, to leave—either school, they wore the colours of both, being striped laterally with light blue and dark blue? It was difficult to tell. . . . (My father had his own views about railway food, as upon many other matters, thinking it excellent, and I recall his saying to me when he was going by train to Renishaw: 'I shall lunch at Chesterfield station. You can't beat it.')

As I was saying, travelling with my father and mother presented its own special difficulties, beginning with the train you caught. My mother always kept her travelling clock half an hour slow, my father his watch ten minutes fast; my father liked to be two hours early for any journey—indeed, my mother told me that on one occasion she decided to be there first, and arrived at the station two and a quarter hours too soon, only to find him already waiting on the platform. Then, in addition, he liked to break the journey unnecessarily at unexpected places, whereas she liked to go straight through to the end and object of her journey. She liked to read and rustle as many newspapers as she could, and, particularly, nearly to miss the train by buying them at the last minute ('Where is your mother? The train is just going.'); or sometimes she would send her maid, who always returned with the wrong papers. My father liked to rest on his round, lifebuoy air-cushion and read about the palaces erected by the Emperor Frederick II, or technical papers such as the *Lancet*, whence he derived his medical theories, subtly changed when passed through his temperament, or one of the architectural magazines and the *Saturday Review* (of the board of which he had once been chairman, when Frank Harris had been editor) or the latest volume on *Leaden Jewellery in the Middle Ages*. My mother would look at the *Tatler* or the *Field*, but liked best to talk on the journey, my father to be silent, except occasionally to administer a snub where it was not needed. In consequence, of later years, they often occupied seats in separate railway carriages and had to be rounded up at their destination by my mother's maid or by Henry or Robins.

Once, when travelling from Scarborough to Renishaw, I remember that our governess decided to take us for a stroll in the station and contrived to become lost as utterly as if we had been in the Green Hell of the Amazon Valley. We got back to the train too late, just as it was snorting out of the station. She then found out that she had not any money on her and was obliged to borrow five pounds from the stationmaster: though why she should want five pounds for that short distance could not be imagined. . . . My own time was spent—as by most children in a train—in screaming and looking out of window, so that I can see that parents also had much to complain about.

One occasion, the most startling that occurred, comes back to me with particular clarity. It took place while the whole family were travelling together. The train was standing in Dijon station when a ticket inspector entered my father's sleeping-car and discovered that our tickets had been issued the wrong way round—from Venice to Paris instead of from Paris to Venice. He threatened to turn us off the train. My father was furious with the inspector—more indignant, I think,

than with the people who had issued the tickets—and I recall
his announcing with a very English accent:

*'J'ai été plusieurs fois membre du parlement anglais et vous ne
pouvez pas jouer avec moi comme ça!'*

Eventually, however, we were allowed to continue our
journey. . . .

My father and mother, as I have said, rarely sat together
of later years but when they did there was no knowing what
might not happen. During the Channel crossing she needed
fresh air and would sit in a chair on deck, while he would
usually lie down and stretch at full length on a sofa in the
stuffiest of the public rooms downstairs. On a hot September
day, for example, we were on the way to Paris and Florence,
and were going to spend the first night at Boulogne (where,
incidentally, when we reached our hotel we discovered that
our luggage had been registered through to Paris). My mother
and father had decided to recline side by side in deck-chairs
placed just near enough to the main gangway to cause
passengers when they boarded the Channel steamer to stumble
over their feet and drop the bags they were holding.

It was one of those sporadically extra-fine days which sometimes descend on the Channel after weeks of rainstorms and
roaring and moaning gales. There were the customary broad-
cast appeals to Mr Spiridion Gentleflower and Mr MacKickle
to report *immediately* to the purser's office—where, one felt,
they would hear no good of themselves. . . . On the other side
of my mother sat a middle-aged couple. They told her all their
history, that their name was Leonard and that they were on
their way to visit the grave of their only son, who had died of
wounds in the first effort to make the world safe for democracy. My mother felt an instant pity for them; especially when
she learned that Mr Leonard had a bad heart, and had shown

[125]

signs of an attack the previous evening. His wife said she only hoped he would be able to complete their tragic expedition. They were to be met at Boulogne and motor straight to the cemetery—about an hour's run. My mother thought that Mr Leonard looked very ill. Emotional and generous by nature, she longed to help. . . . Suddenly she remembered that her doctor had given her a medicine for the heart, which had proved wonderful in her case. She explained this to Mrs Leonard, and they resolved to give the invalid a dose of it at once. My mother sent me to find her maid, and when I had traced her, despatched her to open a dressing-bag and fetch the medicine bottle and a measured glass. The right amount was poured out and administered to the surprisingly acquiescent invalid. . . . The effect had been instantaneous: he became purple in the face, and seemed to swell all over. A doctor had to be found, and the poor man had to be carried below. The explanation was, of course, that his heart normally beat too fast, my mother's too slow. . . . As a result, my mother was terribly worried and angry with the world in general. . . . When we arrived, however, we had the satisfaction of hearing that Mr Leonard was better, and of seeing him drive off. . . .

My father, who had sat there and said nothing to stop what was happening, now spoke:

'Typical of your mother! . . . You'd think that the poor man had suffered enough without being given a heart attack!'

# 16

## A WINK FROM THE GREAT BEYOND

M Y FATHER took what can only be described as a
mystical view of double-entry book-keeping, as if
some unexpected and particular virtue resided in it like a djinn
in a bottle. The world was divided for him into two classes,
the one consisting of those who were at home in this esoteric
language of mathematics and the other of those who were not.
It constituted a test in his mind. A man's character would be
finally summarized and dismissed with the words: 'He doesn't
understand Double Entry.'

My father had an only sister, Florence, two years older than
himself, and it was a great grief to him that she preferred religious
mysticism to material calculation. I could never persuade her to
tell me much about her beliefs. This was, no doubt, my fault
for not knowing how to lead up to the subject, but it was
difficult to do so without committing oneself, and English
reticence also debarred it. I recall an approach on this theme
made to me by a former soldier servant of mine who was apt

on occasion to drink too much. One evening when I went up
to my bedroom I found him sitting on the arm of a chair. As I
came in he did not stand up but gradually revolved on to the
floor, saying with unnaturally precise diction as he did so:
'Excuse me, sir, but do you believe in a Great Beyond?', and
then fell peacefully asleep where he lay. No, that means of
getting close to the subject was forbidden, so I had to be content with other ways. Since my aunt's death I have read and
edited her diaries[1] and greatly enjoyed them. The journal opens
at Renishaw in the 1870s, when she was very young, with the
ingenuous entry: 'George and I have been revelling all the
morning in dirty books.' This, of course, is straightforward
fun, though not meant as such, and intended to be taken
with absolute literalness, but there are further fascinating
entries such as that made after dining at Lambeth Palace
with her great-uncle Archbishop Tait: 'A musical little Mr
Maxwell made a horrid joke about the millennium.' What can
it have been, I wonder? I long to know, for it would seem to be
a difficult event about which to make jokes, whether horrid or
not—no laughing matter, in short. Her journal is evidence
that, however absurd on occasion—curates move through its
pages with, shining on them, the fierce light that today beats
on film stars only—she had a natural gift for writing. She was
also a past master in the art of tantalizing a reader. For instance,
an entry in her journal runs: 'Better news of Claude, only a
bullet through his helmet.' . . . Where was his head, I wonder?
Alas, as the years went by, she became more and more lost in
her private maze of religious theory. Moreover, things so
seldom took the direction she thought—or hoped—they would
take.

In illustration of this: when she was living with my

[1] *Two Generations*, Part II.

Landscape, Montegufoni

The Tower and Baroque Façade. Montegufoni

grandmother at Gosden in Surrey it was her habit to teach a Sunday School class which consisted of gypsy children, among them two gypsy boys. In the first volume of my autobiography[1] I published the following passage from my aunt's journal: '. . . then to our tiny school for the Gypsies which Mother has had arranged in the little wood.' (This sentence inevitably recalls the patter of a music-hall song, usually rendered by a hefty-looking female impersonator:

> My mother said,
> I never should
> Play with the gypsies
> In the wood.)

However, to return to the entry in my aunt's journal:

They [the gypsy children] take such an earnest interest in the simple lessons on the New Testament at the end and now several of them can say a few words of prayer themselves after the lesson. Coralina, aged about fifteen, is, it seems, beginning a true Christian life. Their name is Symes, and they live in a van two miles away.

These words caught the eye of Miss Dora Yates, editor of the Gypsy Lore Society's Journal, who wrote to me and asked if I had any objections to her making enquiries concerning their subsequent development and careers. I was naturally delighted for her to do this. . . . What happened to the truly Christian Coralina I do not know, but Miss Yates was able to trace the histories of the two boys, and found that in early adult life one of them had been tried for murder and the other had often been in the courts for petty theft and robbery. The whole

[1] *Left Hand, Right Hand!* page 236.

[129]

episode is typical of the sort of thing that happened to my aunt and to her religious enterprises.

In her appearance, as in her conduct, my aunt was plainly not of this world. There was about her an atmosphere of submission to the will of God, and her chief joy was to be found in holy books. She had a gentle, early Christian expression on her face, and lovely hair, reminiscent of Mélisande in *Pelléas et Mélisande*. Her old maid used to say: 'Miss Florence's hair is beautiful and golden, and so long that she can jump on it,' which would somehow seem to be a far-fetched and even painful form of exercise for her. Looking back and since reading her journal, I find my aunt a much more interesting character than I thought. Her extraordinary humility and innocence had something wonderful about them, and I recall at my grandmother's the daily family prayers—that now extinct festival—and how her meek voice would sound reading great rolling passages about lions and eagles. She might well in another age have been a saint; except that she was very Low Church and a halo would not have appealed to her nor would she have approved, I think, of saints but only of their saintliness. The great drawback to her everyday existence was her credulity. She believed any story—such as that of the Angels of Mons—which came her way. . . . She never married but at one time she very nearly made a sensational match, becoming engaged to a man who was subsequently tried for murder, which he was alleged to have committed in order to obtain insurance money. He had run a small establishment in Scotland for cramming backward boys, and one youth, on whose life a large insurance policy had been suddenly taken out a short time before the fracas, suffered on the same day a number of attempts to kill him. Of the several methods that had been tried during the space of a few hours, the first was the simple device of pulling out a piece of wood from the bottom of a boat (the young man could not swim) and another of shooting him with a revolver. One of these kindly experiments was at last successful. The case was tried in Scotland and the judgment Not Proven was brought in. But the jury must have been the only persons who felt, or at any rate expressed, any doubt about his guilt. Had my aunt married him, with her vagueness and lack of interest in everyday affairs, he would have found his perfect prey.

I suppose my father was fond of her. At any rate my grandmother's death in 1911 afforded him the opportunity of providing for the use of his sister and her companion two houses—although she only wanted one. It also gave him the chance to enlarge them and to decorate the rooms and make gardens, although my aunt so seldom noticed her surroundings in this world. Of these dwellings one was a Tudor timber house of some architectural interest. It had been bought as an investment in the middle of the eighteenth century by a member of my family, but none of us had ever lived there. In the course of time it had become first a public house—the Flower-de-Luce—and then a farm, and was situated about a hundred miles from Renishaw at Long Itchington in Warwickshire, a village where lived a few of the farming community only. The other suggested residence was just outside the gates of Renishaw. My father laid out an elaborate garden for it, and the place soon became known as 'Ginger's Folly'.

A few days after my aunt's death, her companion saw—or said that she had seen—the ghost of the deceased. The phantom had also appeared to the cook—so it was alleged. The spectre was walking in the gallery of her house in Long Itchington. My father, who usually refused to take ghosts seriously, had chosen to believe this story and said to me:

'Your aunt and I often discussed the possibility of there being a future life. She had probably come back—what is that slang phrase I have heard you use, Osbert?—to tip me . . . ?'

'To tip you the wink from the Great Beyond,' I interrupted.

'Exactly,' my father replied. 'She had probably come to tell me that there is a future existence.'

'Or that there isn't,' I suggested encouragingly.

'No,' he said, 'there would be no point in it. It would mean all that long journey for nothing.'

'In any case,' I protested, 'I'm sure she never winked at anyone in this life and I can't see her doing so in another.'

## 17

## UNUSUAL HOLIDAYS

M Y FATHER had a talent for providing unusual holidays:
though a great part of the fun to be derived from them
consisted in the elaborate preparations that had to be made
beforehand.

It must have been in May or June of the early twenties that
my father, who had returned to England after a stay of some
months in Italy, wrote to my brother and myself, asking us to
meet him at Renishaw. He wished us, he explained, to accompany him on a tour of the tombs of his Sacheverell ancestors in
Derbyshire and Nottinghamshire; that is to say in the churches
of Morley, Barton, and Ratcliffe-on-Soar. He had long planned
such a pilgrimage in the company of his two sons—a ceremony
comparable to the initiation rites that mark the beginning of
adult life in savage tribes—but then the first German war had
come and had cut across the traditional texture of life and
prevented him from carrying out all his schemes. Now that he
could at last put this project into execution, a strange wind

blew from Russia, a new and ice-cold wind, so that the journey seemed remarkable and demoded instead of customary, because roots were mocked at and ancestors were at a discount.

The arrangements he made for this journey were truly tremendous, even though no incident worthy of them occurred during the four long days in which they culminated. . . . When we arrived (yes, it must have been in the month of May, for I recall the expanse of bluebells flowering in every glade and coppice) we found that he was in process of mobilizing the machinery and assembling the backcloths for the unconscious comedy—a comedy big enough to reach over chasms of tragedy—that he could always be relied upon to provide; he had hired a rusty, bumpy motor-car, large and antiquated, he had brought his air-cushion to support him during what he chose to consider the long and tiring expedition before him, while the agile and forthright Robins, who had passed into his service from mine, was darting crab-like through the house executing, so far as was possible in an imperfect world, my father's instructions. . . . My father had resolved to spend the first night thirty miles away at Derby (one could only be astonished that he had not proposed an extra night at Chesterfield, some seven miles from Renishaw). Robins had to pack an array of medicine bottles, the labels on which had all been interchanged, for my father believed that it was the aim of every hotel servant to swallow 'a dessertspoonful, as prescribed', from any bottle that might seem appropriate to the complaint from which they were suffering. If any of them attempted this trick with him now they would get something they had not bargained for—but then my father was frequently his own victim and suffered similarly: for though he maintained that he could identify the contents of each bottle by the look of it, his memory had been known to play him false. . . . There

[134]

were also to be packed quantities of sunset-coloured Thermo-
gene wool against lumbago, whole sets of the very elaborate
system of clothing which he had gradually evolved for himself, mounds of books, most of them in the dingy livery of the
London Library, a mosquito-net from the misty shelter of
which he could emerge to quell possible trouble from the
insect world, many notebooks, the special pens which I have
described elsewhere, and last but not least several luncheon-
baskets containing cold hard-boiled eggs and roast chickens,
iron rations in case we found the towns without provisions. In
fact, the preparations more resembled those that would be
made to withstand a siege than those intended for a peaceable
expedition.

We started in the early afternoon, and from time to time
my father would command the driver to stop, in order that he
could 'rest his back'. This he did by rocking and rolling backward and forward on the seat, so that his companions felt
themselves to be crossing the Channel on a rough day. On our
way, about three miles before we reached Derby, we passed a
signpost with a pointer saying: 'Morley—$\frac{1}{2}$ mile', but to go
there today would, he alleged, be too tiring. So we rattled on
to Derby, where we arrived in time for dinner and, in order to
be ready for an early start the next morning, went soon to
bed. . . . But first my father's bed had to be arranged as he liked
it by Robins, and several boxes unpacked. (Looking at them,
he remarked to me: 'Next time we do this sort of thing I must
really bring enough luggage to make myself comfortable.')
Then the curtains had to be tightly drawn, but proved intract-
able owing to some technical and no doubt permanent difficulty
with the curtain rings. A hotel porter had to be summoned. He
had just come on duty and was very tipsy, so that the act which
he put on with a ladder took an immense time to effect and was

as full of danger to himself as to others. Indeed, it was sufficiently farcical to rank in the Bloomsbury pejorative phrase
of the time as being 'rather music-hall'.

The three days that followed were a series of triumphant
anticlimaxes. It rained all the time. . . . At one place we visited
the house had just been pulled down and there only remained a
square red-brick pigeon-cote, like a truncated tower, which
still bore the arms of the Sacheverells—a building, no doubt,
with an economic purpose: for my father told me as we drove
up how in the Middle Ages the Lord of the Manor could with
absolute impunity train his birds to raid the fields of indepen-
dent farmers no less than those of the villeins, so that the pigeons
grew plump for his table in the monotonous and remorseless
winters of Plantagenet and Tudor times. . . . Then, again, when
we reached what should have been the culmination of our
pilgrimage, the church of Ratcliffe-on-Soar, we found the
floor of the sacred edifice under water, to the height of half a
foot. It was impossible to examine the series of tombs closely
without wading, but from the door they looked, it must be
admitted, impressive and beautiful. Four or five great rectangular masses, fashioned of Nottinghamshire alabaster and
Derbyshire marble, bearing on them the recumbent effigies of
knights and their ladies, seemed to float on a flat mirror of
water. . . . My father refused to be depressed, and merely called
to Robins, who was in attendance outside:

'Robins, another time remember to put in my gum-
boots!'

At last those four days ended, but they certainly ranked as
an unusual holiday. Still more out of the ordinary, however,
was a vacation my father had later, with my aid, planned for
himself—though in the end it had to be abandoned, owing, as
will be seen, to a leakage of information. But first of all let me

recount the singular incident that was responsible for reviving the memory of it.

One year during the thirties I sold our house at Scarborough —Wood End—to the municipality. During the 1939–45 war it suffered damage of various kinds, from the hands of a destructive indigenous generation no less than from enemy bombs. The plain structure in golden stone had stood there for several years with windows void of glass and ceilings fallen: especially the enormous conservatory in the middle of the house looked derelict, an airy ruin of twisted iron frames. To build it up once more must have seemed a difficult and expensive proposition, and consequently some time passed before the Corporation determined to redecorate the house and to bring it back as much as possible to its former style and condition, planning to devote part of the space to a Sitwell Museum and part of it to giving shelter to a collection of stuffed animals—a bequest to the town by the same Colonel Harrison who first brought the pygmies to England from Equatorial Africa.

Five or six years after the end of the war my sister and I drove over to Scarborough to inspect the house, the restoration of which was nearing completion. . . . It was late in August, and we arrived in sunshine, particularly hot and luminous, but scarcely had our feet touched the pavement in front of our hotel before the wettest imaginable blanket of sea-reek enveloped us and prevented us from even seeing across the road to the Town Hall where the Mayor gave us luncheon. After the meal was over we were conducted directly to the Sitwell Museum. The fog had cleared, but as soon as we entered our former home, a brick, inoffensive enough to look at, shot out of the wall at me, hitting the back of my neck and bouncing off it on to the shoulder of the Borough Librarian. There were

only one or two workmen about at the time and they faced
the phenomenon with true British phlegm, but my companions
were visibly astonished and shaken. No explanation of this
incident was ever forthcoming: but subsequently, when I
allowed my mind to run on it, I wondered which, if it were
really a manifestation, of many provocative incidents had been
responsible for such sharp retaliation from the spirit world. . . .
After this manner, then, the memory of an episode that had
taken place at Renishaw returned to me.

It had happened during one of the peerless summers of the
early twenties, when the sun seemed always to shine, and the
scent of box and tobacco plant lay heavy on the air which
carried the melancholy of a long vanished prosperity. . . .
Parents and children were having luncheon together. It was an
ordinary enough everyday British scene—except in one
respect: that the younger members of the family—my brother,
my sister, and myself—were wearing beards, designed by my
sister, and made out of the hideous, lightly tasselled fringe of
an orange-coloured rug; they fastened over the ears with two
loops of tape, and had small bells attached to them, which, with
the movement of the jaws when eating, gave out a melodious
alpine tinkle. These artificial and extraneous adjuncts we had
adopted as an outward sign of compliance and out of respect
for my father's wishes; because one day, not long before, he
had remarked, in a self-congratulatory tone while stroking his
red beard: 'It's a pity that you three children haven't got a little
of this sort of thing.' We could never, notwithstanding, be
certain—since he was as curiously unobservant in some matters
as observant in others—whether he had noticed the new fashion
we had launched on the world that day. Howbeit, during the
course of the meal he had suddenly informed us that there were
to be no guests this year, though he knew we were expecting

[138]

several friends the next day, that it was too late to put them off. My mother, always surrounded by people, but never by so many as she would have liked, looked at him severely with her mournful brown eyes and said, as she had said many times before:

'George, you want me to lead a hermit's life.'

The announcement he had made must have been a disciplinary measure, for we had begun to understand that he liked to entertain at Renishaw—other people's friends, of course, for he had none of his own.

We no longer paid attention to his home-made and favourite maxim: 'Such a mistake to have friends: they waste one's time', because on the evening of the same day he might give vent to an opposite opinion, as when at Montegufoni, pointing to the fragments of a terracotta pot bearing the Acciaiuoli arms on it, he remarked: 'I really must have copies made of that pot, it need not be expensive. I could have them made at Impruneta, or better still Montelupo—it's nearer here, and I could constantly run over there, and give them my advice. As to the cost, I could take six dozen myself for the lemon trees on the middle terrace, and get several friends to join with me and order an equal number. It always works out cheaper if you order a great many. That's the advantage of having friends!'

As always a stickler for facts, I cautiously enquired:

'Which friends are you thinking of?'

I received, snapped back at me, the daunting reply:

'Don't ask unnecessary questions. They'd *all* be only too pleased to be given the chance.'

In short, as he grew older, he became more sociable. When there were guests in the house or when my mother was giving a luncheon-party in London, he no longer had luncheon by

[139]

himself at twelve noon because he found the company tedious; and now, on one occasion, when I complained that one of the guests had told me the same anecdote three times running, he declared:

'I like it: he keeps the ball rolling.'

My father was due, just after seven the next evening, to catch a train to London, there to spend the rest of the week, and one singular consequence of the edict he had thus abruptly promulgated was that from the morning of the following day until he left, the Wilderness—a wood that closed in the garden to the east—became full of figures hidden there as soon as they arrived; friends who had been invited to stay but now found themselves, in order to avoid discovery, obliged to inhabit this bosky thebaid. We had arranged for food to be brought to them at midday, and immediately after my father had departed these involuntary hermits, who remained singularly amiable considering the way in which we had been obliged to treat them, were liberated and dragged in triumph from their leafy refuge to dine with us. We felt compelled, nevertheless, to ask them to leave before my father returned.

During the unfolding of the summer he had become the most wretched victim of his own austere decree. Without guests to amuse him he was in reality immensely bored, though he continually denied this, because boredom (no one had even known the word in the Middle Ages) ranked in his mind as one of the greatest of sins. Although he would not rescind his edict, he felt that something had to be done to combat his ennui, so one morning he sent for me and announced that he felt he needed rest and recreation and to get away for a little (from what, he did not specify); in brief, he must have a holiday, but if possible in some rather remote place, but where there would be plenty of other residents to whom he could talk and who could talk with him in return. He would prefer a house with a fine garden which offered as well a distant view and his bedroom must look over flower-beds. It should be situated in a park with a lake in it—which was to him as running water, h. and c., to those of a more modern and practical outlook. Now as it happened I had only that very morning read in one of the daily papers an advertisement of what was obviously a privately run home for the demented, and was described as 'set in peaceful surroundings with a park and a lake'. Accordingly I told my father about this establishment but did not disclose to him its true nature.

'It sounds just what I need,' he said.

'Well, all I can tell you is that most people, once they've got there, never leave. . . . They like it so much that they've even invented a pet-name for it—"the Bin".'

This appeared to satisfy him, though he added: 'I should like my fellow guests to have hobbies which they could discuss with me, and to be people, too, of some importance.'

'I believe that one of them claims to be a steam-roller, which I suppose in a way *could* be important,' I replied in imaginative frenzy before I could stop myself, 'and another resident maintains that he is the Emperor of China.'

Fortunately, my father never listened very carefully to what was said to him and caught nothing before the last part of the sentence. Indeed, he seemed gratified, and remarked in answer that revolutions usually did a great deal of harm. My brother and my sister also spoke to him of the place with enthusiasm. Indeed, we succeeded in painting for him so attractive a picture of this peaceful retreat that he told his secretary to write immediately for *pension* terms. When the answer came, he said to me: 'Though expensive, it is not exorbitant,' and at once instructed his secretary to engage a room on his behalf for the whole of the month of September. Unfortunately, in their reply, the asylum authorities added to the letter a postscript:

'Ought a strait-waistcoat to be sent for Sir George to wear during the journey, which will be made by van? Three strong and practised male nurses will, of course, be in attendance, and prepared to quell any disturbance on the way.'

This, though it abruptly terminated our design, was by no means the last we were to hear of it. I was packed off to our house at Scarborough, which my father was at that time using as a kind of private Siberia. . . . I was sorry to leave Renishaw in its full August glory, the trees showing as yet no trace of the yellow fingers of the sun, the scent of lilies and stocks lying long on the heavy air, though an occasional gust of wind stirred the tree-tops of the avenue, and left the butterflies clinging precariously to their flowers. Nevertheless, I reflected as I walked to the station, the project had been worth while for its own sake, and my father had nearly enjoyed a long and for once really unusual holiday.

# 18

## CREATING

MY FATHER, as by this time the reader will have concluded, worked himself up easily into an exaggerative state of mind with few or no facts to support this condition. His imagination was wont to catch fire suddenly, but he was more likely to repine and deplore than to rejoice. When at last an auditor would enquire: 'From what are you deducing these catastrophic events that you foresee?' he would take refuge once again in that favourite apothegm, delivered with an Olympian air: '*We happen to know*'. Thus, albeit he was not to be numbered among all those thousands who glimpsed bearded Cossacks with the snow still on their boots from crossing the fringe of the Arctic Circle—yet had he seen them, he would certainly have concluded that they were German troops dressed up as Russians and ordered here specially to nab him (I have elsewhere related how he thought the German Fleet was sent after him to Scarborough when that town was bombarded): nor could he be counted among those later mystics who, so many of them, beheld the Angels of Mons: nevertheless, he too had his visions, but of a depressing order and equally divorced from fact.

One morning in the autumn of the second year of the 1914–18 war, when he was deeply engaged in farming and I was just off to the Battle of Loos—which, incidentally, gave me the idea for my first alliterative entry in *Who's Who*, where, under *Recreations*, I entered: 'Fighting in Flanders and Farming with Father'—he rushed into the estate office, flourishing in one hand a paper of some sort. It was the end of September, the guests were leaving, everything was closing down for the winter, and the family was just off to Scarborough. He was agitated and called to Maynard Hollingworth, the agent:

'I have just received notice that troops are to be billeted in the house. The servants will all leave, and there will be no one to look after anything. It means the ruin of the estate, for they will probably take it over.'

Here Maynard Hollingworth interrupted, saying:

'Can I see the Billeting Order, Sir George?'

My father continued to wave the paper about without troubling to answer Hollingworth. This refusal to let anyone see a paper clutched in his hand was a well-known symptom of his working-up; thus, when he stood there, the document could be seen to resemble that sole shilling that is buried under the foundation stone of some great structure. (These huge edifices that my father built for himself were plainly a form of creation, albeit somewhat gloomy, and it demonstrates what a useful thing slang is, for the slang use of the word 'creating' expresses perfectly the mental processes. 'Sir George is creating this morning something terrible!')

Maynard Hollingworth reiterated: 'Isn't that a cheque in

Montegufoni from under an Olive Branch

Stone Lion, Montegufoni

your hand, Sir George? If you'd let me look at it I might be able to help.'

My father made no attempt to reply or to give it him but went on adumbrating his dream of destruction.

'There is no knowing what may not happen,' he continued. 'The books in the library will all be burnt, and no doubt my Family History, which has taken many years of work, will disappear. The stables will be pulled to pieces, all the trees in the park will be cut down for firewood. . . .'

Later in the day Hollingworth contrived to obtain a glance at the paper. He found it to be a cheque in payment for the billeting of horses in the stables which had ended a month before he received the document. . . .

My father was later deeply distressed by the Government's granting permission to Lord Cowdray's firm, S. Pearson & Son Ltd., to bore for oil on the Sitwell estate just outside the park near Foxton Wood. Accordingly, he permitted himself to be persuaded by the general manager of the neighbouring coal mine that oil could be reached much more easily and quickly in Eckington Woods, also on Sitwell property. The reader will not be surprised to learn that after reading a single pamphlet on oil my father had become a self-decreed expert on it. ('Such a pity not to consult *me* before they started work.') In a few days he sent a telegram to Lloyd George, who was by then Prime Minister: 'Have I your permission to bore for oil? Can reach it months before Cowdray.' He received no reply.

On the other hand, nobody ever struck oil there, though Lord Cowdray's experts drilled through the coal measures, and through Mountain Limestone and Millstone Grit, only at the end to be faced with brine. . . . Creating, in its other and opposite form, now began. When he heard that brine had been found my father remarked that they would soon have to abandon the site and perhaps he would be able to build a health resort, similar to Harrogate or Droitwich, and inaugurate brine baths as a cure for arthritis. 'The men who built Bath as a cure town made a fortune,' so he told me when I next saw him. 'The doctors, I know, will be enthusiastic about it, and I could go to Lutyens for the plan of the town—luckily, he has had plenty of practice with New Delhi—nothing too ambitious, just a group of stone nymphs and another group illustrating the Seven Ages of Man, but in an opposite order from that in which they generally appear, so as not to depress the patients unduly. First of all there would have to be hotels and shops. These could easily be built within a few months after the war ends. The doctors would all be housed in a separate quarter. (They would enjoy being together.) Then there would have to be an arcade for patients to walk in on rainy days, and the nature of the ground gives ample opportunity for me to make a fine garden for them. Nothing rheumatic patients enjoy so much as being able to sit in a garden. It needn't be big—about twelve acres. . . . Then there is the question of the swimming-bath itself. It should be two or three hundred yards long with an arcade and made of scagliola. And the Opening Ceremony—what would you advise for that?'

'I think you should dive in to open the pool,' I suggested.

'Yes, that would amuse my friends, but I'm afraid my diving days are over'—and they certainly were. None of us had ever known him to swim.

# 19

---

## A RAP OVER THE KNUCKLES

R EADERS of my autobiography may recall that upon one occasion, when I was occupying the next bedroom to my father's at Renishaw, I woke up in the small hours to hear his voice declaring in a very sinister manner: 'They May Think I Shall—But I Shan't!' This pronouncement was followed by a prolonged chuckle. Now whether these words were spoken in his sleep or when awake I shall never know, but certainly they describe and define very precisely an attitude he often struck in his conscious hours. Indeed, 'They May Think I Shall—But I Shan't' ranked with him as a game, and one which, I believe, he was proud to have invented. First, you led your opponent on by niggling and worrying him over what course of action to pursue in a particular quandary and then, just as, after a fever of fussing, you had induced him to think that you had settled on a specific line of action, you switched off that plan and on to another, which would then have to be argued all over again from the beginning.

My mind reverts especially to one instance of his using this very personal technique. It occurred sometime during the few enchanted years just before the First World War, when summer appeared as if it would last for ever and each hour showed its own special glow and lustre: when Clio, the Muse of History, had apparently settled down to a placid middle age, and the only events she produced would turn out to be menus of pleasure. Such disputes as existed were the result of particular political problems such as Home Rule for Ireland, Lloyd George's Budget—always afterwards referred to as *The* Budget, as though no other had ever been brought in—and that child of The Budget, the Veto Bill; a bill intended to curb still further the powers of the House of Lords. This, apparently, could only be effected by Mr Asquith, the Prime Minister, advising the King to create at once a large number of Liberal Peers—a large enough number to pass the measure—but they, alas, always showed a most retrogressive tendency to adopt the Conservative creed, however much they had denounced it previously, the moment they entered the august precincts.

Many people were much concerned about these matters, my father among them. He had at last recovered from a long illness and was full of energy again. As usual he constituted himself, as it were, a self-elected one-man government. Continually he wrestled in his mind with this problem; what, in particular, could be done to defeat the machinations of the Liberal politicians? although himself had recently, and publicly, adopted the Liberal faith! At last his ingenious mind found a way out. Accordingly, he wrote to the Conservative chief, Mr Balfour, and in spite of personally holding the poorest opinion of him, whom he regarded as little more than a half-baked philosopher, an amateur esthete unduly fond of music, with none of the qualities of a leader, and as a man who had founded

[148]

his position on the support of numerous influential relations and of a particular set in the social world—my father, in short, wrote to Mr Balfour to tell him that he had thought out a plan by which Mr Asquith's threatened action could be averted, and wondered whether the statesman would care to know about it. After a day or two an answer arrived stating that Mr Balfour would indeed be very interested, and asking my father if he would write to him and communicate it. My father then just wrote back, no, he would not; a prime instance of 'They May Think I Shall—But I Shan't!'. . . . Probably Mr Balfour in his vagueness hardly registered the rap inflicted, for truly he was very absent-minded. (Did he not during a luncheon given at Claridge's by a transatlantic hostess, pass to me under the table a note which ran: 'Can you tell me the name of our hostess and where she is sitting?'; a classic instance. . . .)

Another of my father's favourite phrases was: 'He needs a rap over the knuckles', such as the one administered below. He had a habit of discussing the high political questions of the day with his secretary and asking for his opinion on them. One day his secretary said to him at last: 'How can I advise you about such matters, Sir George, when you know far more about them than I do?' and my father replied: 'It isn't *your* advice I want. I need to hear somebody else's view, it doesn't matter whose, so that by a process of contrast and comparison I can more clearly formulate my own opinion.'

If my father's principal motto was 'They May Think I Shall—But I Shan't!', my mother's, obversely, and though she would never declare it in words, was 'They May Think I Shan't—But I Shall!' . . . There comes to my mind a particular instance of what I am trying to indicate. . . . One cold winter my father decided to move from the country into an hotel in Florence: it would be warmer and he could economize: my

[149]

mother would not be able to entertain so lavishly nor to give such large parties as at Montegufoni. After a week or so at the hotel my father suffered one of his recurrent attacks of imaginary illness and resolved to move again; this time into the Nursing Home of the Blue Nuns for a month.

When he mentioned this decision to my mother he was rather surprised to find her in such a co-operative mood, for usually she would insinuate that his illnesses were hypothetical: but on this occasion she told him that she thought he was quite right to take his indisposition seriously, and so, after having given a valedictory exhortation to the strictest economy in his absence, he was wafted off in the Ark the same evening for a month's rest on the sunny heights of Fiesole. . . . There Henry would bring him up the English papers every afternoon—but one day they were late. In consequence, one of the nurses, feeling sorry for my father, confined as he was to the reading matter he had brought with him—*A Flutter Through Manorial Dovecotes in the Sixteenth Century, Over the Border, an Account of Flodden Field, Wool-Gathering in Nottinghamshire in the Dark Ages, Rotherham before the Norman Conquest, Medieval Fools, a Study of Court Jesters during the Wars of the Roses,* and *The Stone Age on the Yorkshire Moors*—took pity on him and brought him a weekly paper, printed in French and published in Florence in the cause of tourism. It was devoted in the main to most favourable accounts of local social events and to fascinating lists of the guests staying in the various hotels—a paper which he had not seen before and probably would never have set eyes on at all if Henry had not failed him on this single occasion. My father opened it at random, and the first paragraph that caught his eye was headed: 'Lady Ida Sitwell gives a fête at the *Hôtel Ali Baba et Macheath*.' The account of it said that Lady Ida Sitwell had offered a dinner to forty people in honour of the visit of her

[150]

sister Lady Mildred Cooke. (It did not say, however, how shy Lady Mildred was, nor how much she must have hated it.) Then came the menu of the dinner, the names and order of the wines and liqueurs, and an account of the table, decorated with pink roses that had been specially flown from the Riviera. It was fortunate that my father was already in a nursing home, for certainly this information would have sent him to one, in order to recover from the shock of the announcement of my mother's determined stand for economy during his absence. . . . The feast occupied his mind for weeks. In the list of *convives*, as the paper called them, occurred the names of all the best-known *pique-assiette* in Florence, and I remember his telling me that when the bill came in and he queried the amounts charged for liqueurs, he was informed that some of the guests had ordered full bottles of brandy and Cointreau and other imported liqueurs to take home with them. . . . Henry Moat was the person who suffered most: for not having told my father about it. He ought to have known, my father said. It was disgraceful of him.

'But I heard nothing about it, Sir George.'

'Well then, you ought to have found out.'

'But how could I, Sir George?'

'Don't argue, it stimulates the brain cells and prevents me from sleeping.'

## 20

---

## POPULARITY

IT WAS in May 1923, when tenants who would not
be moved were still many of them living in the Castle,
that my father asked me to go for a walk with him in the
Great Court. The summer heat, which in certain years
begins in Tuscany as early as the second week in May,
was not yet in full glow and the shafts of sunlight, instead
of piercing like spears, lay light as feathers on the dark
stone of the pavement. Even from this distance, too, the
bees could be heard swarming in the dark-leaved golden
blossoms of the ivy which completely covered the stone
medieval tower at the garden's end. As we strode up and down,
my father talked, I remember, of the translation of books, and
remarked to me what a pity it was that if the English Bishops
of King James I's reign had felt obliged to translate a volume of
some kind, they could not have found for their purpose a more
interesting book than the Bible. I did not attempt to enter into

argument with him as I did not think that it would lead very far. Occasionally, as he talked, the shutter of an upper window would silently shift a little, and a face would be seen framed in it, glowering and glaring down at us. My father seemed pleased, taking it to be a token of interest and popularity: indeed, he observed to me that it was nice to feel that you could always make yourself liked if you wanted to. But facts have an awkward way of asserting themselves and when, shortly afterwards, an old woman was arrested by the police, she was found to be carrying on her a list of people whom she meant to kill when the Revolution came: my father's name was at the head of the list. Yet even if his assumption had been rather too sanguine, there were fragments of truth in it. He could make himself generally and lightly popular with great numbers but had no gift for intimacy. Thus he would be popular at a large meeting rather than in talking to an individual as a person. In this respect I think the house-to-house canvassing that was formerly conducted in between general elections by the candidates of both parties must have been a great strain on him, for he had difficulty in remembering people (as I have written elsewhere, he would frequently pass his own children in the street without recognizing them) and, if he remembered them, in associating them with their names. Thus, on one occasion he went into a small house under the Castle Hill at Scarborough and asked a woman who was ironing shirts to obtain for him her husband's vote. She looked at him and said: 'But I am *Mrs Jones*, Sir George.'

This information conveyed nothing to my father. He did not identify her as the wife of his personal servant who had been his scout at Christ Church and had remained with him to serve him ever since. (He was butler when Henry Moat first came to us as footman, a day which Henry always lamented as being the last on which free beer was provided in the servants' hall. He used to say: 'I joined up too late.')

A more obvious instance of the falsity of my father's happy conviction comes back to me when I think of my first visit to Chiswick House. It proved a memorable occasion and took place in the early twenties when the building was still in use as a private mental home. It was necessary beforehand to obtain permission to go over it from the Commissioners of Lunacy, who kindly granted my request. Accordingly, my brother Sacheverell and I went there about four o'clock one hot afternoon in July. The house, built for the great patron Lord Burlington by Colin Campbell, then existed, of course, on a larger scale than it does today, when the two later eighteenth-century wings have been blown up or pulled down to show the purity of design of the original Palladian villa. . . . We were to have tea with the resident doctor, but on arrival we were not certain by which of the doors to enter. However, we opened one of them and there, coming down the staircase, was a good-looking grey-haired man already wearing a dinner jacket—it seemed an odd hour to be clad in this manner. We enquired from him where the doctor lived and he replied by whistling, but—and this was the most extraordinary part of it—the words were absolutely distinct, yet enunciated by—not through—the whistling. He was, in short, whistling and not speaking. It was obviously a natural and original gift, though he must have cultivated it, too, to the highest degree and surely must have been the only person who could communicate in this way. In addition, had he so desired, it would have placed him among the most highly paid stars of the music-hall stage. This virtuoso, then, informed us that we were on the right track. . . . When we reached the doctor upstairs, we found a most splendid and impressive tea ready for us, sandwiches very thinly cut and bearing flags on them, cut out of paper, on which were written such descriptions as PÂTÉ DE FOIE GRAS and CAVIARE. My brother commented on this smart labelling to our host, who asked:

'Did you happen, when you came in, to notice the whistling man who was wearing a dinner jacket?'

We said: 'Yes.'

'Well,' he explained, 'he arranged the tea. He always does it for me. A most curious history. His father was one of the Marshals of France during the reign of Napoleon III and a great favourite at court. His son inherited a fine fortune, but dissipated it on prima donnas. I had known him for a long time, but some ten years ago we received a letter from him telling us that he felt he was going off his head, and asking whether we would take him in here to be under my care, in return for which he would act as a servant—but every now and then he asks permission to go out for the evening and the next day we read in the *Morning Post* that he was at some social gathering to which I should never be invited.'

It was, as I was saying, a peculiarly sultry day and after tea the doctor led us through the suites of rooms which, richly decorated, with gilded cornices and painted ceilings, formed a strange setting for the wretched lunatics, all over-excited by the heat. Many of them shook as if with fever, and their faces were yellow from the glow of the gilding as much as from illness. You could hear cries and roars and screams on every side. When we had completed our tour we went out on to the platform at the top of the staircase leading down to the garden. The vista was a perfect instance of the esthetic beauties caused by neglect. It was not a flower garden, but a large pleasance, though owing to the skilful planning it looked immensely larger than it really was. An idyllic rusticity prevailed, aided by the greensward, stone vases, pools of bracken and groves of old trees. We wandered about there for a while and talked. Then, as we turned to climb up to the portico, we saw approaching a tall, lank man with an air of some distinction, who carried over his shoulder a bag of golf clubs.

'Oh, I am so glad,' the doctor remarked to me, 'that this particular patient has come out. He must be on his way to the golf course. I'd like you to meet him. Don't feel the slightest alarm: he has never been violent and is a very charming person.'

The doctor beckoned to him to join us and he was formally introduced to me.

'This is Mr Osbert Sitwell,' the doctor announced.

'Are you Sir George's son?' the lunatic at once demanded.

I admitted it, and before you could say Jack Robinson—or whatever other proverbial name you use to describe the swiftest passage of time—his demeanour changed and, rather hastily selecting a golf club, he shouted: 'Then I should like to kill you.'

By some means or other the doctor persuaded him to disarm and go away without any of us incurring injury. But it was a breath-taking moment. Having successfully spirited the patient away, the doctor hurried back to us, saying:

'Oh, I am so sorry! What a dreadful thing to happen! He has never been known to behave like that before.'

In that same instant I recalled my father striding along in the Great Court at Montegufoni, and the faces peering down at him, and I wondered by what precise act of his I had so nearly, if vicariously, shared his popularity. I never found out.

## 21

## NEAPOLITAN STREET SCENE

IN THE autumns of the years immediately following the
First World War my brother Sacheverell and I would
sometimes join my father and mother at Naples, where we
would stay at Bertolini's, a hotel like a ship that floated on a
hill half-way between the heights of Vomero and the city
below. The hotel possessed a good deal of character. You entered it at a level considerably lower than the body of the
hotel itself, through an opening in the rock face, a little resembling the so-called Tomb of Virgil at Posillipo, except that
after you had walked to some depth inside, you found a lift
which soon whirled you up to the hotel public rooms, situated here above the bedrooms, and to terraces that recalled the
decks of a ship. At all hours, terraces and windows offered an
unparalleled view of grandiose but dilapidated palaces, and of
the domes of churches striped in herringbone patterns of
yellow and green tiles, and set among palms and orange trees.
At times when the wind was in the right direction the noises

of the city, so unlike those of any other in the world, would mount to one sound, a characteristically vital and yet sinister diapason. . . . Moreover, each month offered its own features: thus one day in mid-December, during one of the visits to Naples, I walked to the Piazza Oberdan and saw there two men disguised as clowns of a sort striding on stilts which brought them to the same height as the tip of the marble Guglia, and then entering the church found two shepherds playing on bagpipe and wooden trumpet, serenading the Virgin in her *presepio*.

My father enjoyed staying at this hotel, albeit he considered it rather expensive; he did not, however, like the bread provided. Therefore it was one of Robins's duties to go every afternoon to Caflisch's, a café and bakery in the Piazza dei Martiri below, to purchase rolls for breakfast the next day, but when he asked at intervals for money on account in order to pay for them, I always noticed a drop in paternal enthusiasm.

A particular instance of this, when my father, Sacheverell, and I had walked down to the town, comes back to me. . . . It was a golden October afternoon and the whole town glowed with its own vital forces as well as with the heat and noise of what seemed a summer day. As we neared the Piazza dei Martiri the tide and force of sound was amazing; this hymn to life was composed of the music of barrel-organs, of hoarse voices shouting and singing, as well as of the conventional cries of the men who presided over the stalls in the piazza; stalls decorated with tufts of pampas-grass, where they sold peeled Indian figs, piled in pyramids, ready to be eaten, showing the colours of a blood orange, water-melons, the scarlet flesh of which was exposed, peppered with large black pips, and drinks made from fresh oranges and pomegranate juice. Further, there were the sad oriental groans and moans of the beggars, still in those days to be encountered in great numbers haunting popular corners and parading their infirmities. . . . Into this scene my father fitted well, in spite of his fair skin, prominent nose and red beard; indeed, I remember thinking he a little resembled Captain Fracasse or another one of the figures of the Italian Comedy. . . . At the end of the Via Roma we met Robins looking very worried. He touched his hat, came up to us, and said to my father:

'I was hoping to catch you, Sir George. I'm on my way to get your rolls for tomorrow, but I haven't a penny to pay for them. Could you let me have a few *lire* on account or I don't know what I shall do?'

My father did not answer directly to him, but observed to me in a voice calculated to be very distinctly overheard:

'Disgusting, I call it, stopping one in the street and asking for money like a beggar!' He then walked on, angrily humming to himself—but the rolls were there the next morning.

# 22

## LORD HENRY

LORD HENRY was my mother's first cousin, though he seemed to belong to a much earlier generation, and, indeed, must have been much older than she, for when he had sat in the House of Commons he had been one of that handful of young aristocrats chosen by Disraeli to be trained and ready to hold high office in the future. Besides, *he* had really belonged to the days mentioned before in these pages, when in the drawing-room after dinner men would sing ballads; and the music of one of the worst and most popular of them—'O Dry Those Tears'—as well as of several others less celebrated, had been composed by Lord Henry. . . . He never, in fact, attained the position in politics predicted for him, because a personal scandal of a non-explosive order—if a scandal can ever be non-explosive—had wafted him to Italy when he was twenty-eight, and he had never returned to England. However light and almost private the scandal may have been, it had, of course, proved sufficient to blast the life of everyone connected

[160]

with it, although my mother and the members of her family would hear no word in his dispraise.

Eventually he had settled down in Florence, where he built himself a house—or, more accurately, an elaborate and, taken all in all, rather hideous little palace in one of the styles associated with King Ludwig II of Bavaria (so that perhaps he saw himself as being his own Wagner—but with what a difference —to his own 'Mad King'). Everything that could be gilded —and much that could not—had been gilded. Nevertheless, the house was fascinating, for it was full of personality, and it was clear that a great deal of thinking had gone into its planning and into the contrivance of every detail. In so far as the house possessed a theme it was that of family pride. The coat-of-arms, much in evidence, was that of the Plantagenet Kings and still displayed, as well as the Lions of England, the Lilies of France; a claim discarded for his successors by King George III. Otherwise the house was a pure experiment.

In the Tuscan spring you entered from a whirl of dust and dry fallen blossoms of wistaria and lilac blown by the hot wind into spirals, to find yourself in a gilded oasis of tall potted palm trees and carved pillars. There were among the clusters of rather small rooms that composed each floor some designed to look larger than they were by the aid of various structural stratagems and decorative tricks: others offered their own inherent interest. One room, for example, had an inner ceiling resembling a canopy supported by gilded pillars and was enclosed by transparent walls of plate glass. (When one day I asked my cousin why he had built it in this way, he had replied that he had always wanted to know what it would be like to sit in a room without walls.) Another room had yellow walls that, when the electric light was turned on, changed their colour to a tone of rosy copper. The house was crammed with precious and decorative objects, but contained few pictures; of these the finest was a panel by Bernard van Orly.

The occupant and owner of this house was very tall, six foot four, and to his last days never stooped but held himself absolutely erect. To look at, he resembled a very well bred pelican and he also presented a certain likeness to Don Quixote, which was emphasized as life drew progressively further away from him. As he grew older he seldom went out, but feeling at last that he should have more fresh air, he had caused a motor-bicycle and side-car to be built to his specifications. He had carefully planned the whole matter: the machine must be controlled by one of his menservants, and himself was to sit in the side-car, but—and in this consisted its originality—the side-car was built at right angles, instead of being parallel, to the motor-bicycle. He had arranged for it to be made after this fashion in order, he explained, not to attract attention. Alas, it did not have that effect, but produced quite an opposite result. The start was quiet enough. He had intended to ride up to the heights of Fiesole, but somehow or other he never reached them. Dressed as usual in a dark, well-cut suit and large-brimmed hat, he wore invariably, indoors and out, a pair of carpet slippers on which were emblazoned his initials in gold thread. He was not, in any case, of the sort of build or appearance that would be associated with a side-car: but this side-car, in which he sat with his long legs stretched out in front of him, proved irresistible as a popular spectacle. Word had somehow gone round and the streets were lined with an appreciative, indeed rocking, crowd. After a short hour he was forced to abandon the machine and he never used it again.

As he grew older Lord Henry felt himself to be out of

sympathy with the age that was clearly shaping itself, and the affair of the motor-cycle confirmed him in his prejudices. Towards the end of his life this was manifested by his never going out at all and by his moving up a storey a year, until, finally, he could rise in this world no further above ground level. You would find him ready to receive you in a large, ornate bathroom at the top of the house dressed in a cowled white bath-robe and wearing on his head a biretta of purple silk propped up and kept in place by a small lump on his forehead. Here he would be ready at six o'clock to give his visitors a cup of black coffee—never tea, for tea he forbade to be brought into his house, since, he would explain, tea-drinking was 'responsible for all the terrible scandal talked in English drawing-rooms'.

In these later years how Lord Henry spent his days I cannot imagine. He cannot even have sat in the garden, which was a dark tangle of laurel leaves and very umbrageous plants, so overgrown that there was no room to move, though it looked cool and refreshing when seen through the windows. There did not seem to be many books in the house. He would, however, write every day and receive in return a diurnal letter from an old lady. This correspondence went back to the days when he left England: but what they can have found to write to each other about is beyond comprehension, for each hour that passed was increasingly empty of events. To his visitors, Lord Henry liked, after the manner of all old people, to dwell on times past. He would talk about Disraeli, or mimic him—an imitation which those who remembered the dead statesman would say was very true to life—or he would describe how himself would walk away from the House of Commons very late and suddenly feel a small arm hooked in his. It would be Lord Beaconsfield on his way home after speaking in the

House of Lords. Lord Beaconsfield would invite Lord Henry to supper and, when they arrived, they would find Lady Beaconsfield, bejewelled and in full evening dress, waiting as always for her husband. Lord Beaconsfield at first seemed too utterly exhausted to open his mouth, but directly his lips had touched a glass of champagne he would revive suddenly and become again the brilliant person he was. . . . Lord Henry also liked to tell us about d'Annunzio, who was a friend of his.

Lord Henry's ivory tower was very different from that my father had through the years constructed for himself; though both were alike in the failure of their original purpose —to find total refuge from the present day and the future. . . . My father, rather unexpectedly, liked Lord Henry, who, he said, had the best manners of anyone he knew, though being in essence an art and cultivated to the highest degree, they were perhaps a little over-elaborate and formal—but my father's regard for him did not prevent Lord Henry from giving, or my father from receiving, one or two jumbo-sized snubs; a process to which my father was not used, being accustomed to deliver them himself.

The first time I saw my cousin was during the Easter holidays from Eton which I spent in Florence in the year 1908. He had invited us to dinner. We arrived punctually in spite of the delaying tactics of my mother. My father rang the bell. Immediately, an oblong piece of metal slid away from an aperture in the door and a dark eye was visible looking through it. Apparently the inspection was favourable, for the bolts shot back, and the door was thrown open by two servants dressed seemingly as wrestlers in jerseys with alternate blue and red lateral stripes. We entered and were conducted by a footman in livery to the Glass Room in which our host was waiting for us. After we had greeted him he led us to the Blue Dining-

[164]

Room, reserved for guests of royal blood, or at least with a drop of it in their veins. At the side of each guest was a gold case full of Turkish cigarettes. (I was greatly flattered by this compliment to my years.) I now think, looking back, that these cigarette-cases must have been made by Fabergé, but at that time I did not know the name. The dinner was excellent and everything, including the ice, but excluding the young turkey which was the main dish, bore his coat-of-arms on it. When dinner was finished and we were drinking our coffee, my father turned to Lord Henry and asked:

'Why do you have that silver-gilt statue of King Arthur in the middle of the table?'

'Because I am descended from him,' Lord Henry replied syllogistically and with an air of finality.

My father had to accept this, though he was a well-known debunker of pedigrees—including his own—for he held that genealogical truth was of more interest than any invented descent. But what could he say against this bland assumption? He could neither retort: 'You're a liar', nor even: 'I think you are mistaken.'

## 23

# MUSIC

I NEVER knew my father to go to a concert in spite of his liking for 'a little music after dinner'. He regarded it as the least important of the arts. It was not practical and you could not touch it. Even painting, he used to maintain, was a more useful art because you could often gather from the pictures, for instance from those of the Florentine and Sienese Primitives, the most interesting facts about contemporary life in the thirteenth and fourteenth centuries, how the people dressed and what they ate and with what implements. The facts that he gathered were submitted to a well-known process. He would not divulge them, but would probably 'keep them up his sleeve' for the future. (The reader may perhaps recall that on one occasion my father said to me: 'Between ourselves, I have the whole history of the two-pronged fork up my sleeve,' and on another: 'Between ourselves, I have two miles of lead-piping up my sleeve.') Further, music gave the patron —to whom rather than to the composer or the executant, the chief glory in his opinion was due—little opportunity to show off. He had, he would protest, many *useful* things to do. He could, for example, go round to the College of Arms and worry the Chester Herald about the Barons of Pulford, or he could look up in the British Museum fascinating details about life in Rotherham under Cromwell, full of helpful hints about economy. (The household bills were a revelation.) There also always remained the Black Death to study if other subjects failed. Whereas music was of no practical use whatsoever. Therein he was wrong, as I will show.

For example, in 1923 my sister, my brother, and myself were staying in Munich. By chance this visit coincided with that of our intermittent friend Siegfried Sassoon. I had apparently in some manner unknown to me succeeded in annoying him so that, as happened not infrequently, we were for the moment not on speaking terms. Hearing that he was to dine one night at a fashionable restaurant to which we were also going and which had a band, I persuaded the conductor to watch me and at a prearranged signal to strike up the March from *William Tell,* knowing that the strains would go to Siegfried's feet, as it were, and compel him to march in time to them through the whole length of the restaurant to his table in a distant corner. . . . The moment I saw Siegfried enter I gave the signal to the conductor and we watched the victim advance in a procession of one to his table exactly as planned. After that it was difficult for him to be so very dignified and in consequence the temperature of the whole dispute was lowered. . . .

Few restaurants, I suppose, now supply their own music, but there is always the radio or a juke-box to take its place. In the hotel—a monastery until the suppression of the monastic orders—in which between the wars I used to spend the winter months in the company of various friends, there was a band which played by fits and starts—mostly, one would have presumed, by fits. The winter patronage of this long white building, which fitted into the cliffs high up on its wall of rock, was in the main exercised, not as at one time by a steady resident population, but by parties of passengers from boats bound on pleasure cruises. They were not much used to travelling. (I recall a member of one of them opening a conversation with me by saying: 'There seem to be a lot of Roman Catholic churches in Italy.') The party would arrive from Naples by charabanc. Directly it had left that city for the Salernitan Gulf—to travel at horrifying speed—especially, it seemed, round corners—along the coast road between, on one side high limestone cliffs where jonquils grew in every crevice and cranny, and on the other side a precipitous fall with the sea coloured like a peacock's tail lapping, or occasionally roaring, at its base—the manager would be informed by telephone that a party was on its way. He would then in turn send messages down to the members of the band, telling them to cast away their cobblers' lasts, to abandon the cutting out of shirts and the clipping of hair and climb up the long steep flights of steps to make music for the pleasure crusaders.

The music supplied—'Santa Lucia' ad lib. and the odiously sportive and lubricious 'Funiculì, Funiculà'—was abominable. The band consisted of five men in all. The barber played a mandolin, while the cobbler blew into a pitcher, thereby provoking a deep and dull reverberation. In front of these men, a little girl wearing a pink dress was stationed who would sing very nasally, making peculiarly rigid and conventional gestures, first with one hand and then with the other, expressing nothing. Such an entertainment might have afforded the entrancing rustic fun of Pyramus and Thisbe in *A Midsummer Night's Dream*, or of the music of the *Società Filarmònica di*

[168]

*Montegufoni;* a group composed of peasants and shepherds playing in a superbly pastoral setting: but it did not. By those who were to be borne away on a ship the same night, it may have been thought to be characteristic or to rank as a piece of debased local colour, but to those making a long stay in the hotel it became insupportable and nauseating. Something had to be done about it.

With the more than willing support of the friends who were of our party, I arranged a plan. At luncheon one day, when a charabanc company was present, we waited until the band began to play a near-'Santa Lucia'—'Santa Lucia' itself was too well known for our purpose—and then abruptly rose to our feet and remained standing in the tense manner associated with national anthems. The guests, though puzzled concerning what country it could be that had adopted this tune, were anxious not to hurt any national feelings and hastily rose until the whole company was on its feet. The band was flabbergasted. Its members had played the tune hundreds of times without anything of this sort ever happening. What new nation had come to birth in the last few days, they asked themselves? The little girl in front was so startled that she forgot to make her gestures, and the members of the band were taken aback to the degree that one or two of them even played the right note. They had, they must have felt, inadvertently trodden on a national anthem.

Thus it can be seen that music has its uses.

# 24

---

## MAGIC

As a child the toys I most enjoyed playing with—and in this I think I was typical of every child—all had about them an aura of the inexplicable. Thus I was specially fascinated at the Guy Fawkes season by the magnesium tapes which when burnt turned into the likeness of a coiled serpent, the dried pieces of paper from Japan that resembled dirty matchsticks but swelled into highly coloured flowers when immersed in water, and even a simple magnet shaped like a horseshoe with which to pick up steel filings, or any puzzle that made use of that alchemist's liquid metal, quicksilver, never to be made fast. But if I liked to be astonished, my father, I believe, liked to astonish; even his own small children; and when I was four or five he used to make magic for me by causing a penny to disappear from his hand, and by shaping with his fingers and with the aid of a light the shadows of rabbits and cats and goats upon the wall. I was immensely impressed by these achievements and my mind was very much occupied by them. I can recall easily today the tall, authoritative man that he then was. Sometimes he would come to visit me on his way down to the drawing-room before dinner, when he would be wearing full evening dress. This must have been at our Scarborough house: but at Renishaw he was able to produce a piece of magic which for me outshone all the others. . . . I would be playing in the garden when I would hear him suddenly call my name from a distance: then, looking up, would see him waving at me from between the battlements on the roof. How did he rise to that altitude, by some process which many years later I learnt to refer to as levitation? How did he get there? I wondered, rather in the style of the well-known question attributed to King George III, who, when faced with an apple-dumpling, is supposed to have asked repeatedly on one occasion: 'How did the apple get *inside* the dumpling?' It never entered my head that he could do anything so prosaic as just climb a staircase. I did not find this out until a year or two later, but when I did discover it, his prestige suffered immensely in my eyes: because, from being a sorcerer, he had sunk to being a mere conjurer, and sleight of hand was shown to have masqueraded as magic.

Nevertheless I took a great fancy to the roof myself, and the door, on the third storey, of the wooden staircase that led to it was conveniently opposite a nursery. By the side of the staircase stood a large dappled rocking-horse, which had been drawn a century before by Octavius Oakley, showing my grandfather holding, and two of his sisters riding it, the elder girl dressed in the manner of some Cruikshank drawing with knickers showing beneath her short skirts. I was not, of course, aware of this at the time, but I knew that I was forbidden to ride the rocking-horse myself, on the score that a great-uncle of mine had fallen off it and had been killed: whether this was true or an improvisation by my nurse, I never found out; but if it was an invention it was outstandingly successful in frightening me, and nothing would have induced me to climb on its back. Conversely, it seemed impossible to keep me off the roof for long. By stretching, I could just reach the handle of the first door leading to the little wooden staircase and with more difficulty the handle of the door at the top, within one of the three gothic spires, leading to the roof itself. The keys had been lost, so there was no difficulty about locking or unlocking.

I made the expedition twice before I was caught. I was supposed to be resting after luncheon, but in the manner of all children my one idea after a meal was to rush round the room at tremendous speed and never to stop running, jumping, and singing for hours. So my nurse, on the first two occasions to which I refer, had been puzzled to find it much easier than usual to persuade me to lie down, and when she saw my hands at the end of my rest she could not think how they had got so black. Though she had been in the next room, she had heard nothing, so quiet and careful had I been. As I have said elsewhere, her favourite motto was: 'Even a slave has an hour for his dinner', and she might have added 'and another hour for digestion', for that was the amount of time she liked. . . . But the fiasco of my third visit to the roof was entirely my own fault: if I had not acted foolishly, I should again have reached home safely. It was a particularly fine day, however, calm and full of sunlight, and the roof was fascinating; the best place possible from which to seize the beauty of the whole lay-out, the counterpoint of light and shadow, of water and dark yew hedge, and from which to look down on the golden mounds of the tree-tops. The roof also afforded an easy way to compute the age of the original house and the various additions to it; for the part with stone tiles belonged to the time of King Charles I, and the grey-blue slates to different periods in the eighteenth century, while the chimney-stacks also afforded their clues. Of course, I did not realize this at the time, but the beauty of it, of the light and colour, excited me and seems to have warped my judgment. By standing on the flat part of the roof and stretching on tiptoe, I could just get my head over the gap between two battlements. Everything looked beautiful. Suddenly I saw my father walking across the lawn alone. Overcome by the feeling of my own cleverness in reaching here unaided and by my pleasure at seeing him, because he was usually indoors at this hour, I determined to give him a pleasant surprise, and shouted as loud as I could: 'Father! Father!'[1] I saw him turn round immediately, look up, and then begin running towards the house. What I think chiefly frightened him was the thought of the wooden planks which led from one ridge to another. It would be easy for a child to trip and fall over, and the valleys between the ridges were often very deep. I was happily playing in the sunshine when the hasty tread of feet on the creaking stairs announced his arrival, accompanied by my nurse, who on this occasion wore the woebegone expression of a saint in a picture by some Flemish artist such as Roger van der Weyden, and a flustered nurserymaid. I was carried downstairs kicking, and put to bed. My mother, however, did her best for me as soon as she found out what had happened, pointing out to my father how lovely the day had been and how playing in the rare sunshine of our climate could do me nothing but good. . . . I did not quite understand what I had done, but whatever it might have been, I regretted it because my nurse and Jenny were in disgrace,

[1] To some of my readers it may seem strange that I called father 'father', but the more intimate 'daddy' belongs to a later generation, as the use of 'papa' and 'mamma' belonged to a generation earlier.

though my nurse never blamed me for it. She was, however, usually in disgrace with my father, because she had been nurserymaid to my mother, and any faults my mother had developed in his eyes were attributed to her regime.

There was staying in the house at this moment one whom my father considered more culpable still, my nurse's exalted guest, Mrs Ayton, who had been nurse to my mother and her sisters. Indeed, in a sense my father was right, for if Mrs Ayton had not been there and had not been immersed in conversation about nameless scandals (nameless because it was her belief that if you omitted to refer to the persons of whom you were talking by their full names, but only in some way indicated them, then it did not count as scandal at all), my nurse would have heard me moving about. . . . Mrs Ayton may have been the villain of this piece, but she enjoyed the widest esteem in the world of the Housekeepers' Rooms of the country houses she went to: and she settled herself annually for a full month on my mother and each of her three sisters. She had now retired and lived for the rest of the year with her three children —two daughters and a bachelor son—in a small house at Balham. She was an old woman with grey hair, worn out-of-doors under an old-fashioned bonnet decorated with sequins, and she found her chief pleasure in talking. Upon her upper lip grew the ghost of a grey moustache, always moist from tea-drinking, which made being kissed by her a horrid experience; but for her faults she would atone by bringing with her always a special kind of chocolate cake of which she alone knew the secret recipe. She seemed to me very ancient at that time, but she lived another twenty years to be ninety-one and to be bombed out of her house in one of the comparatively rare air raids in 1917. Indeed, preparations against air raids became the chief interest of her life in later days, when she could not visit my mother and her sisters since country houses, if not all shut up, were not in a state to receive anyone. Directly an air raid announced itself, she would get up, dress, and sit near the kitchen fire surrounded by her children, talking about the event—ample scope for her conversation—and waiting for the end, and on one occasion the end had nearly arrived. All that my father said when he heard of her misfortune was:

'So like her!'

## 25

## THE ROCKING-HORSE

IT MUST have been in the autumn of 1935 that I was dining with my father. He seemed in a jaunty mood that evening, and asked me—which was unusual—what sort of day I had spent.

'A singular day in two respects,' I replied, and began to tell him what they had been.

In the morning I had been listening to the speeches of the orators at Marble Arch. I had watched the solitary figures coalesce into crowds and then the crowds gradually disperse again. As I had turned away from the particular clump I had joined, it was with the accustomed feelings of disappointment and dissatisfaction. The words of the speaker, floating on the air, followed me.

'Only co-operation can save the world,' he was saying.

The slogan might be true, I had reflected, but as a programme it seemed somewhat vague.

'Co-operation can be a disaster,' my father objected.

The Grotto, Montegufoni. The Goddess Latona

The Grotto, Montegufoni. Peasant throwing a stor

'In what way?' I enquired.

'Look at our coalition governments. Always when this country is in danger there is an outcry to have a coalition. The idea is, I suppose, that it's safer to place your life in the hands of two fools rather than of one.'

I resumed and told my father how I had been thinking about co-operation when I reached the Serpentine. Then I had turned along by the water's edge. The day and the place were beautiful, elegiac with fallen leaves, wraith-like mists, and the scent of bonfires, the flames of which flickered like gonfalons on a light breeze. I had reflected how melancholy the people looked who passed, whether lingering by themselves or even in companies—but suddenly there had been an abrupt change to another tempo. Faces broke into smiles, feet into runs rather than walks, movement in general became lively and bustling. The centre of this cheerful commotion was the bridge, just as the sun which had come out was the centre of such heat as there was. The feeling was one of liveliness and expectation. I had wondered whether the crowd had gathered here to watch a film star go by; but then I noticed that all the faces were turned outwards towards the water. The cheerfulness was now such that complete strangers talked to one another. What could it be, I asked myself, that had caused this stir? A man pulled me by the sleeve and said:

'Have you seen the suicide, they've just found the corpse? He's there, under the blanket.' . . . So that was it.

Looking down at the lake, I saw an oozing mass under a sodden brown army blanket on the asphalt path. The water spread out, trickling over the hard surface. . . . It's difficult to know what governs such matters or what will make people talk, but a shock of some sort is patently required.

The second unusual incident had taken place in the

afternoon in the toy department of one of the big London stores.

I was choosing a kind of game and in reaching up to a shelf to get something which the assistant thought I wanted, upset a pile of light flat white cardboard boxes on to a stranger's head. I knew they weren't heavy enough to have hurt him, but still it must have been annoying. I had noticed him when I came in, a rather distinguished-looking man examining a rocking-horse. . . . I apologized profusely, and then added:

'That's a fine rocking-horse you've got your eye on!'

'Yes,' he said, 'I'm buying it as a birthday present for a small son. I'm determined that he shall have the toys of which the children of our generation were deprived.' . . .

The shower of cardboard boxes seemed to have melted the ice.

He spoke English with a slightly foreign intonation, no accent, but the rhythm of his speech wasn't English. He talked in rather a formal way.

'What good English you speak.'

'Do you think so? I'm afraid I talk like a book, for all my English was first learnt by reading. Are you the writer?' he went on.

I admitted it.

'Well, I'm the pianist Boris Michaelis,' he said. 'I don't know whether you've heard me play, but your books have given me great pleasure. When you've finished your purchases, perhaps you'd come and have a cup of coffee with me downstairs and I'll tell you more about the rocking-horse.'

I looked at my watch and finding it was only four o'clock accepted the invitation. When coffee was brought he said to me:

'I'll tell you something about myself, a subject about which I usually speak little, but as an author you'll understand. I was born and brought up in Cernauti, or Czernowitz, as it is now, in Rumania. This town was formerly a centre from which quite a disproportionate number of creators poured through to Europe and America. My father combined the rather contradictory professions of music teacher and impresario, but he was a poor man. I worshipped him. He had designed my career directly I was born. His aim was to produce me as a virtuoso pianist and from the very first I was trained to be, and in fact was, a child prodigy. I gave my first concert in Czernowitz under my father's auspices at the age of five. It had all been extremely well organized and the hall was crowded with genuine musical enthusiasts, as well as with kind ladies who doted on children. At the end of the concert there was tremendous applause, and it rose to a climax when a huge rocking-horse, brilliantly dappled, was carried on to the stage by two men and presented to me. Children up to the age of seven have little self-consciousness and, as a child would at that age, I clambered on to the horse the moment it was put down, and began to rock. That was certainly the greatest moment of my childhood. I had longed for a rocking-horse as far back as I could remember. The applause doubled and increased to the volume of thunder. It was a triumph, though I say so myself, and earned great praise in the local Press, which compared me as a virtuoso—for such I was—with Mozart at the harpsichord at a similar age. As for me, the rocking-horse claimed all my attention. I didn't respond much to the applause, but felt I could go on rocking all night. I was soon rushed home, however, given a bowl of soup, and sent to bed. I wanted to have the rocking-horse stabled in my bedroom so that I could rock to my heart's content the moment I woke, but my father wouldn't allow it to be put anywhere except near the front door. I wondered why, as I fell into a sleep of exhaustion.

'Though I was woken early by a van arriving and driving away again almost immediately, my first thought was of the rocking-horse. I went out into the passage, to discover that my toy had vanished. . . . When later I discovered what had happened—that it was all a deception, that my father had hired the horse for the evening, and that I should never see it again —I lost all my great love for him, and from then until today the very sight of a rocking-horse has made me feel sick—or it did until I chose that one upstairs for my boy.'

My father gave all the well-known symptoms of being displeased, fidgeting and flickering his eyes sideways. I often made the mistake of expecting an ordinary response from him.

'Of course, his father was quite right,' he said, 'in sending away the rocking-horse. He couldn't afford it, and was determined not to encourage the boy in extravagant habits. It would have been much more sensible if he had been able to save up and later obtain for his son a commission in a good English cavalry regiment.'

'But he wasn't English,' I objected.

'Well, no doubt the boy could easily have got naturalized,' my father remarked. 'He could always have consulted me. I'm afraid I've no patience with him.'

# 26

## MAKING A BOLT FOR IT

M Y MOTHER died in a nursing home in London on the 12th of July 1937, and in August my father left England for Switzerland, and thence, after a month's visit, returned to Montegufoni. For the long stay he proposed to make there he had provided himself with some companions—acquaintances, it must be admitted, more than buddies—and others we had found for him, in order that he should not be lonely—or, to be precise, not more lonely than the complete suit of armour he had grown for himself in the past half-century rendered inevitable. In it he was now ever encased impenetrably, the vizor down, so that he revealed his face only a little less seldom than his hand. In addition, I had told him that I would join him in Italy whenever he wished, but I became aware in talking to him that he was not really eager for me to do so, because he liked to be in a position of absolute command, with nobody to gainsay him, and since I, too, was accustomed to having my own way, this encroached on his prerogative. However, during the course of a few weeks he came to cherish a certain sense of grievance, most carefully nurtured by various of his acquaintances, at his children not being round him, and towards the end of November, some two months after his return to Italy, telegrams were suddenly shot at me from all sides with such vigour and poignance that they inevitably recalled the multitude of arrows that pierced the writhing body of St Sebastian. This barbed shower revealed behind the shafts a formidable power of organization. They sped from people young and old, men and women, worldly and unworldly, Italian and English, prelates and laymen, but all united to tell me that my father was very ill and that it had now become my duty, however disagreeable, to be at his side. I at once took the train for Florence.

On arrival at the Castle I found arranged for my benefit a tableau, a death-bed scene like one of those that occur in the paintings of the Italian Primitive masters. My father lay in a four-poster—baroque in style, I must confess, rather than gothic —receiving fruit, fresh eggs, game, and sympathy—but not flowers. These last he rejected outright because they were prone to give him hay-fever. . . . As I entered the room, the figures relaxed and the tableau broke up. My father proceeded to dismiss the guests with a little ceremonial flutter of the hand, and went on to tell me at once of his serious illness, although there were no outward signs of it in his physical appearance. I therefore asked him to be allowed to talk to his doctor, Giglioli. He gave me permission, and accordingly I bumped into Florence in the Ark, described at some length elsewhere, to interview this sympathetic and most intelligent Italian doctor. When I asked him if my father was very ill, he replied:

'The disease which Sir George assumes he has developed is

a matter of X-ray plates and not of faith alone. He is an old man of seventy-seven years of age, and of course if he gets a cold it may always turn to pneumonia: but probably he will outlive me and be with us for another twenty years.' (My father did in fact survive his doctor by some five.)

On my return from the city I found the invalid still in bed, and looking intensely depressed. As I opened the door of his room, he enquired in a drooping voice:

'How long does the doctor give me?'

'About twenty years,' I replied.

At this he suddenly jumped out of bed with an agility that would have done credit to a man half his age, and said: 'I must dress now.' That night he came down to dinner.

The long journey and change of climate had afflicted me with a bad attack of lumbago, and the next morning I had breakfast in bed, and was therefore rather late in making my appearance. First, from a small room above the Cardinal's Garden, protected from the wind, and full of late November sunlight, of roses and stocks and of drowsy butterflies in the last florid stage before their hibernation, I had observed my father holding court in a deck-chair—or rather in the kind of long wicker chair that he liked because he could put his feet up and thus rest the heart, and one of which was always reserved for him in any garden that he owned. He reclined on these hard open-work planes of wicker at the top of a flight of steps commanding the view: the valley of vines, and nearer, climbing the Castle Hill in steep terraces, the long tank-like stone beds full of blue plumbago, leading up in turn to the surrounding box parterre, in which were growing the flowers he had chosen for it in pale, pastel colours. . . . Round him were grouped the courtiers. . . . There was a man with more false teeth in one mouth than I had ever previously seen gathered

[183]

together, and rather ill-balanced they were, too, so that his conversation was an act of perpetual conjuring. There was Signor Bracciaforte, smiling as always, full of childish benevolence, easily moved to tears or laughter. There was a young girl, a student of history, her figure slightly foreshortened by fate and a-clink with the old paste jewellery with which my father delighted to hang it. Her eyes, I noticed, seemed to be perpetually full of tears and she had a sweet smile of sympathy showing from a head hung rather on one side. There was another girl, a cousin of ours, and then there was my friend Francis Bamford, who had kindly offered to accompany my father to Italy and to look after him. (To him my father had in the past months uttered some of his more sudden, startling, and Delphic warnings and aphorisms, such as 'Never be Kind to a Dowager', and 'One can see in my grandchildren how Nature is trying to reproduce *Me*!')

When I got downstairs—with some difficulty—and appeared in the garden under that cloud of awkwardness that always overshadows the latecomer, I said: 'Good morning, Father.' He greeted me in return and then gave a significant, rather ominous glance at those round him from under eyelids that seemed to work sideways rather than up and down; a signal which the court knew from experience was calculated to convey dismissal. Watching in silence till his guests were out of earshot, he remarked to me in a voice of unusual dignity and importance:

'Osbert, I wish to speak to you alone.'

I replied rather carelessly:

'Then I'll get a chair and sit by you. How delicious it is out here, Father! This is the first sun I've seen for months.'

To my surprise, for he usually liked to warm himself in the winter sunshine, he answered:

'No, I would prefer to speak to you in the Gothic Library.'

He proceeded to lead the way to the small, cold, high room, which I have described earlier in the second part of 'Unforgotten Feasts', on the north side of the house. On the faking of it he had for some years been engaged, spending on the process a very considerable sum of money. It was, of course, a library without books—I say of course, for it could always be noticed that, though he loved books and lived surrounded by them, none the less in any room which he called a library no single volume was ever to be found. At Scarborough, similarly, his library had been bookless, though each of his several sitting-rooms even had books piled up all over the floor. But this library was, its very appearance proclaimed, a State Apartment, to be used solely for giving audiences and making special pronouncements. No book had ever been brought into it or was ever likely to be, and people, it was plain, seldom entered it. Indeed, it proved difficult to do so. First you had to find your way down some break-neck steps set at odd angles at the bottom of a spiral staircase, and then to get yourself through a doorway forbiddingly narrow, like a coffin. When finally you reached the room, it had a recess lined with cypress-wood cupboards. Too shallow to hold books, they were crowned with a flat, gothic fretting as cornice, and their panels were edged with a margin of leaves, rabbits, and human figures cut in very flat relief, expertly carved. The detail of the presses, lightly touched with colour, and of the vaulted ceiling, disproportionately high, had, if I am not mistaken, been derived from one of the nine canvases by Carpaccio, depicting the life of St Ursula, to be seen in San Giorgio degli Schiavoni in Venice. The cupboards had below them, attached to their base, seats that resembled medieval instruments of torture; although, as if in mockery, they were thinly padded in places with flat cushions, soft stone pancakes, covered in blue and silver velvet. Herein and hereon we sat, the two of us facing each other, for the cupboards took up three sides of a square. We bore our discomfort manfully, pretending not to notice it. I can see my father now, as he sat there, very upright, with the sun through the barred window catching the gold glint of his red but greying beard. He was wearing a grey suit and one hand rested on a cushion. In his manner could be perceived, by one familiar with his ways, both a certain air of tension and a wish to surprise. Thus I was prepared for something portentous—and sure enough it came.

He gave a slight bow and said:

'I thought I ought to inform you, Osbert, that Mrs FitzDudley Gudgeon wishes to marry me.'

This unusual announcement winded me. I had seen Mrs FitzDudley Gudgeon. She was a widow with no background but a past, and a past of peculiarly unpleasant character, who had for half a century and more trailed behind her a long train of unsavoury financial transactions merging into love affairs, and vice versa. . . . She had contrived to cultivate my father's society for some years. Once at a concert at the Queen's Hall she had come cringing up to me in the interval, and had said: 'I know your father'—to which I had replied: 'Yes. Better than I do, I believe.' But most clearly I remember the first occasion on which I had seen her. It was at a party, and I recall it vividly because a friend of mine, much older than myself, who had been standing by my side, had turned to me as she entered the room, and had said:

'Here comes the wickedest woman in Europe.'

This had naturally focussed my attention on the neatly dressed, discreet-looking, grey-haired woman who entered. What he said might be true: but here was, I found out, an

[186]

unaudacious, flat, mousy, money-grubbing kind of wickedness without any endowment of wit or wits, and lacking in the fun that sometimes attends and makes lively the company of sinners. It demanded a guaranteed sound return, and constituted a real four-per-cent-preference-share brand of evil.

Naturally, I had noticed my father's unusual choice of words. So now I asked him:

'Do *you* wish to marry *her*?'

He replied: 'I am not certain, but she has written to me to say that she would like to come here for a long stay.'

'Well,' I enquired, 'what will you do if she insists on marrying you, and you don't want to?'

'Make a bolt for it, I suppose, as I had to once before. . . .'

Recollecting previous conversations with my father, I seized immediately the implications of this gallant reply: because, when I was younger and he had been fond of warning me of the dangers of everyday life, he had often related to me how, when just down from Christ Church, he had arrived to stay in a famous country-house for a ball. The two daughters of his hostess would be great heiresses; but unfortunately, though he liked them, and they, so he claimed, entertained feelings deeper than friendship for him, yet my father disapproved of both the young ladies: for he considered that they were over fond of pleasure, and feared, moreover, that they might like to spend money too freely. Another motive influenced him even more profoundly. As I have related before, he held very strict views on eugenics, and their noses too nearly resembled his own in shape (so he had told me), and this, if he had married either of them, might have tended to accentuate the aquiline profiles of his offspring, and so have deprived his children of the classical mould of feature for which he hoped, and which indeed he was determined, to secure

[187]

for them. . . . It was difficult to follow precisely what happened. Howbeit, so far as I could make out, on his entering the hall a footman as usual had taken the heavy leather portmanteau with which a man then always travelled—when, to his surprise, he had discovered that the heiress who was his particular friend was waiting for him there as well. Her presence at once convinced him that the young lady expected him immediately to propose to her; indeed, beyond the hall lay a vista of rooms, and at the end of it the conservatory door could be seen open in invitation. He had felt it imperative, if his children were to avoid nasal catastrophe, to act at once. Therefore, hastily snatching back his luggage from the footman's arms, he had pelted back down the drive and through the park without offering to anyone a word of explanation or apology, either at the time or subsequently. . . . This—though I may have gathered some of the details incorrectly—I could have no doubt was one occasion on which he had been obliged to 'make a bolt for it'. . . . But that was nearly sixty years ago, and at the moment I was concerned with stopping the threatened alliance. To take first the most obvious of present difficulties, plainly he would not be able to run so fast at his present age, while Mrs FitzDudley Gudgeon was quite capable of running after and catching him! The best way, I concluded, of preventing the marriage was to find for him a rival attraction to Mrs FitzDudley Gudgeon, because obviously he felt a need for feminine sympathy and for presenting himself in a new light and as a centre of interest. What could be done? Fortunately my mind lighted on Mrs Rippon: a woman of character and humour and formerly a celebrated beauty; a pirate, but kind and audacious, and of quite a different sort. . . . He liked her, and her husband was rumoured to be dying. Accordingly I improvised.

[188]

'Well, I must admit I always saw a different future for you,'
I remarked.

He said: 'What do you mean?'

I replied: 'After Colonel Rippon's death, I thought Ethel
Rippon would marry you.'

At this he looked very pleased with himself, and I realized
that I had defeated Mrs FitzDudley Gudgeon's scheme once
and for all.

.        .        .        .        .

There is little more to add, except that after my father's
death, when I returned to Montegufoni at the end of the war,
I found among his papers all the correspondence that had passed
between him and Mrs FitzDudley Gudgeon—for he kept and
filed copies of letters he wrote, as well as preserving those he
received. Just as the letters quoted in the Bardell *v*. Pickwick
Trial were said by Serjeant Buzfuz to have been written
in code, so that an order for 'Chops and Tomata sauce.
Yours, Pickwick', conveyed the declaration 'I love you',
so these unusual *billets-doux* were couched in the current
technical terms of the English and European, but especially of
the American and Canadian, Stock Exchanges. It was easily to
be deduced: the tenderness of Mrs FitzDudley Gudgeon's
requests for information about Abitibi shares and the prospects
of Brazilian Traction spelt ardent and everlasting devotion for
my father and the respect she cherished for his wisdom—still
more for his wealth: while his affectionate response to these
demonstrations took the form of such phrases as, 'I hear
Beralts may pay a bonus' or 'I advise you to stick to Chinese
Customs 1882.' Moreover, alas, I am bound to conclude that
the counsel he gave her in his final communication, to avoid

[189]

further 'flutters' and to invest all her 'loose money' in Consols, constituted both a reproof and a call to order, equivalent in that language of love which they had evolved for themselves to the words: 'Let us part on terms of friendship; I wish to be let alone, and have no intention of marrying you.' After that, there came no more letters.

## 27

## THALIA

M Y FATHER had made a bolt for it—or, rather, his
mother had made it for him—once before, a year or
two earlier than that just described. . . . The opening scene of
this bolt is set at Renishaw, but it was a very different place
from that of today: since my father had not yet had time to
begin the numerous improvements which, in spite of many
plans started and never concluded, he effected there during the
following half-century: the yew hedges had not been planted
yet, nor had he built the terraces of the formal garden with
which he was to re-establish and increase the beauty of the
immediate surroundings: nor was the magic mirror of the lake
below yet in place to double the prospect of trees and sky; these
were all to be begun some ten years later. I do not remember
the landscape garden which he destroyed: and it is difficult for
me to construct it in my mind. A fine green lawn, over which
flower-beds were dispersed for no particular reason, swept
down in front of the house from the Avenue to the Wilderness.

The house, my father told me, seemed unanchored to the ground it stood upon, though the lie of the land must always have been magnificent. I once asked my great-aunt Blanche—whom readers of my autobiography may remember—what the garden was like before the changes, and she said: 'Renishaw had always an enchantment about it.' . . .

Everything indeed seemed golden, everything was at its brightest and best in those particular days at the end of May and beginning of June in the early eighties of the last century. My father had just come of age after a minority of nineteen years. So capable a woman had my grandmother proved herself to be that she had contrived to pull the estate together, and by the end of this period to pay off the heavy debts contracted many years before my grandfather had succeeded, and which had for long been such an encumbrance. The old ship was afloat again. Everything looked golden. My grandmother still presided over the house for her son, and at Church of England services rich and poor alike joined in the singing of hymns with such words as:

> The rich man in his castle,
> The poor man at his gate,
> He made them high or lowly,
> And ordered their estate.

Everything seemed golden, and even my grandmother, though apt to take a dark, dramatic view, did not discern through the golden mists of the eighties and nineties the ruin that was in the next generation to descend both on the houses of this kind and on the way of life to which they gave shelter. . . . For several hours a day my grandmother would rest on a sofa, her face, with its melancholy smile, a mask of Christian resignation. This

[192]

year she, together with my aunt Florence, had presided over a succession of parties—lasting much longer than the Friday to Monday visits of today. Florence, her only daughter, had never, I apprehend, been of much help to her in mundane affairs, her head full, as it was, of the approaching millennium to the utter exclusion of all else. Charitable and ineffably religious, my grandmother had been obliged for the time being to become worldly—but at least she could still enjoy putting away all secular books on a Saturday night in preparation for the intensive all-in religious wrestling to occupy the next day. Every party over which she had presided had been based on a sound foundation of religion and family relationships, and had culminated in the visit of Archibald Campbell Tait, Archbishop of Canterbury, guardian and great-uncle to my father, and who thus belonged to both worlds.

His visit, however, was over, but the house was again full of guests. It is not necessary to name and describe them all here, but they must be kept in mind as a background to the action. The relations present, in addition to my aunt Blanche, included a cousin of my father's, Hildebrand Sitwell, who proudly filled the position of black sheep to the family—in those days every county family possessed its own black sheep—and to whom my aunt Blanche was in consequence much attached. Black sheep could always count on her sympathy and affection: and there was nothing in which she so much delighted as helping a lame black sheep over a stile, though the effort would sometimes require all her strength, tenacity, and love of fighting. On this occasion, moreover, Hildebrand had come here to introduce his new betrothed, named curiously Thalia, and to show once more that he had turned over a new leaf—for though still young, twenty-six—he had become an almost professional turner-over of new leaves.

Thalia, to whom he was now engaged, was dazzlingly pretty and everyone liked her immediately for her appealing looks and charm. On this visit the couple had already spent ten days here, and were expected to stay another week. But fate decreed otherwise.

Thalia seemed to like everyone and, in short, liked my father so much that she made a declaration of her feelings to him. It is always, I believe, difficult for a girl to isolate a man from his surroundings which, in her mind, have become part of him, or to separate from him his achievements and possessions. Thus it is unfair to deduce that a girl has married a man because, let us say, he is Prime Minister. To her the man and his office are one, so that the quality of enchantment mentioned by my aunt Blanche as always belonging to Renishaw had been in part responsible for Thalia's switch-over, as well as the fact that here was a distinguished-looking young man in a preordained, Meredithian mist of golden fortune and destiny.

My grandmother's version of what occurred dates from many years later, but had by no means shed the romantic lustre with which her turn of mind had invested it, and by her manner of speaking which those relations who did not like her —and there were not many—would have characterized as 'affectation'. Be that as it may, she had, so she said, suddenly felt—owing to what was known then as 'a mother's intuition', but would now be called 'E.S.P.'[1]—that my father needed her help, though she could not tell in what connection. So she went straight to his room, entered it, and found him with his head in his hands 'in an attitude of, oh, but despair!' She gently asked: 'George, what is the matter?'

He replied: 'Mother, Thalia has proposed to me.'

[1] Extra-Sensory Perception.

[194]

'But, George,' my grandmother pointed out, 'Thalia is already engaged to Hildebrand.'

'Yes, but this morning she broke off her engagement with him and told him that she had fallen in love with me.'

My grandmother soon had the situation in hand. She had chosen from the background a friend and contemporary of my father's—subsequently to develop into that quaking, cultured Silver Bore who, as I relate in *Laughter in the Next Room*, was to cost me in the future a galleryful of Modiglianis—and had swiftly arranged for him to set out at once for a walking tour with her son. It was to occupy ten days. (This was, nevertheless, essentially a bolt for it, though rather longer and slower, and covering less distance, than was to be expected.) Meanwhile, Hildebrand had declared his intention of shooting someone, either himself, Thalia, or my father—or, better still, all three together—and, carrying with him an unloaded revolver, which had, however, no bullets with which to fill the cylinder, had proceeded to lock himself into the box-room, where he brooded for several hours. What the other guests thought, I do not know, but my aunt Blanche, of course, championed Hildebrand and gave expression to the opinion that 'George has behaved disgracefully', a pronouncement which, when repeated to him, was one of the main reasons for my father's subsequent life-long feud with her. It was my aunt who eventually persuaded Hildebrand to join the outside world once more for dinner, though when he had come out most of the party wished he were in again. This she accomplished by saying brusquely: 'Come out of there, Tom!' (she would never call him Hildebrand) 'and don't be such a damned donkey!' . . . Later he settled in China, and was no longer able almost professionally to darken doors in London. (The injunction:

[195]

'Leave my house, sir, and never dare to darken my doors again' was still in current use in the eighties, left over from and popularized by mid-Victorian melodrama. Indeed, sons and lovers would have felt deprived of something if they were spared this admonition. The next step would be the threat of a horsewhip.)

My grandmother had spoken quietly to Thalia and persuaded her to return home in two days' time. During this interval my grandmother and Thalia were much together and took their meals upstairs in the boudoir. This propinquity through many trying hours was responsible for a mutual friendship, improbable though it may have seemed at this juncture, especially in the present circumstances for which Thalia was plainly responsible. Thalia now officially broke off her engagement to Hildebrand and even promised my grandmother to lay off my father, in fact not to see him again.

The last chapter of the story took place some twenty-five years later, one spring in the Boltons; the Boltons, that late Victorian haven, nebulous island of houses and gardens and dogs, of church spires showing dimly through the fog, that floating island, so solid when you are in it, so difficult to find when you are looking for it—perhaps because it survives in its own separate pocket of time, different from that of today. . . . Be that as it may, my grandmother had bought a house there in the last years of her life, and one day when my sister was staying with her, my grandmother told her the postscript to the story, with its unusual choral culmination.

After two years had passed Thalia married an English officer in an Indian cavalry regiment. From India for many years she kept up a regular correspondence with my grandmother. . . . Her life, I think, had not been very interesting. Indeed, the most unusual feature of it was the number of children born of this marriage. Eventually, the entire family had come home to England for a brief visit.

My grandmother asked them to tea. . . . I can imagine the scene, the drawing-room full of the sunlight of a May evening in London, in which the silver cabinet glittered and the gilded rococo chairs—now in the next room to that in which I am writing—glowed. It must have seemed to her when Thalia entered the drawing-room, as if she were leading a procession, a well drilled procession dwindling in height, which gave a false perspective to it, making it look even longer than it was. When the children were all drawn up in single file to be introduced, my grandmother related how Thalia had remarked:

' "Mother"—for she always called me Mother—"would these were George's": and the Dear Nineteen joined in, chanting: "Yes, Mother." '

## 28

## THE NEW JERUSALEM

O F A fine evening in August during the twenties, after a
solitary and early tea, my father—wearing a light-
weight grey suit, and brown brogue shoes rather too delicate
for country mud and for the wet tufts of rank grass near the
water—liked to walk down to the lake and round it, in order
to see how the plantations he had made were prospering, and
to examine the distant views revealed by the fellings that had
taken place. As a younger man, he would have been found at
this hour paddling along in a canoe, with Monarch, a black
spaniel, following behind in the water at a discreet distance,
though one from which he could still splash his master if he
wished, or even try to board the boat and succeed in swamping
it. But Monarch was long dead and my father now preferred
to walk round the lake. Sometimes he would ask me to join
him. We would descend the flight of steps in the middle of the
garden and then go through the iron gate at the top of the hill.
At this season, the yellowing grass was close-cropped and the

only flowers in the park would be drifts of harebells with their translucent blue cups swinging on invisible stalks, clumps of toadflax in their two tones of yellow and jungle tangles of convolvulus engaged in gradually strangling the green bushes on which they climbed: but in spite of this nefarious procedure they produced large white trumpet flowers having an air of unusual innocence and beauty. Partly running down the hill, for it was so steep that it impelled us to run, we reached the lake through a thicket of wild raspberries. Here at the water's edge was an entirely different set of flowers, fragrant clumps of lilac-coloured wild mint, the clustered spires of magenta loosestrife, and, just inside the banks, groups of meadowsweet and bulrushes. On the water itself, in the middle of the lake, two kinds of yellow lilies floated, one a large round-petalled nenuphar with a red centre resembling the inside of a pomegranate, the other a small yellow flower, insignificant except for the abundance of its blossoms, but the leaves of both formed big golden circles floating on the darkness of the water. . . . A difference was visible, too, in the insect world: here the dragonflies darted and skimmed: it was too late in the year for the great quantities of azure dragonflies which were to be seen in July, though a few might survive, but it was those of a larger species which now attracted attention as they sped on dark gauze wings in dry crackling flight. Their bodies were brown and varnished or marked with green, blue, and yellow like a grass-snake's belly, their eyes protuberant and endowed with more facets than man has ever contrived to cut in the largest and finest diamond. Occasionally a kingfisher would flash by and, more rarely, a heron would be seen fishing in the marshy part of the lake opposite Half-Moon Plantation, having flown apparently some forty miles for an evening's sport, since the heronry nearest to us was at Kedleston.

My father walked very fast and, as was his wont, would stop suddenly—abruptly enough, indeed, to make anyone walking behind him collide with him—and raise binoculars up to his eyes in order to obtain the distant views. Sometimes we would cross the path of a trespasser, a miner off work for a day or two and engaged in gathering a bunch of wild flowers to make into a posy to compete at a local horticultural show, where there would be competitions in flower arrangements: and very pretty the bouquets would be, with flower heads of each sort, pressed together in concentric, concolorous circles; very pretty and unexpectedly fastidious, with their contrasts of texture, of the lacy interweaving cow-parsley and meadowsweet contrasting with more robust flowers, and reminiscent of the bouquets clasped in the hot hands of bridesmaids, dressed in early-Victorian style, at fashionable weddings. It seemed odd that miners, after their heavy work, should indulge in such fragile and elegant fantasies, but in those days people made their own amusements and were happier for it. . . . My father would not notice the interloper, his mind being occupied with other matters, and distant enough to bring out sometimes a real surprise. Thus one evening, suddenly interrupting himself in the middle of explaining how unselfish of him it had been to make all the improvements he had effected here—lakes and plantations and a drive through the wood—for the benefit of generations unborn, he looked up at the hill and, forgetting what he had said, just pronounced:

'This wicked taxation will most probably drive you out of England, in which case you must emigrate to Canada or America and build a copy of the house there: but though I shan't, I fear, still be here to help you and the architect with my advice, I can give you a few tips now. The new Renishaw must be an exact replica of the present house and garden, except in one respect: the stones needn't be numbered and moved one by one across the Atlantic, nor need it even be built of the same stone: but you must find a position for it with a natural resemblance to the original site.'

I was floored and stunned by the outlining of these new measures of economy.

'How am I to pay for it?' I asked.

'You must keep expenses down in every other direction. It needn't cost so much: it would be unnecessary, for instance, to make the lake at first. You could wait for that until you had settled in the house, then you could keep an eye on the work yourself.'

'But what I want to know,' I reiterated, 'is how I am to pay for the purchase of the site and for building a house?'

'As for that, there are always the Building Societies. I understand they exist, as their name implies, for the purpose of encouraging building. They'd be only too pleased to help, I imagine. It'd be a real chance for them. Now you'll see, my dear boy, why it is so important to be economical in small things. The pocket-money you have enjoyed might have come in very useful, for a shilling a week soon mounts up at compound interest.'

'It's too late to do anything about that now, I'm afraid,' I said rather unsympathetically. 'The question is, who is going to find the money for everything?'

'I have already told you—the Building Societies. You may have to draw on the resources of more than one of them, of two or three perhaps, but of course they'd jump at it. It's the sort of opportunity they don't often get.'

'The building operations you suggest are not of the kind that the directors would support,' I objected.

'Then they've no right to call themselves *Building Societies*,' he replied crossly. 'It's a piece of imposture. I never heard of such a thing. But of course you're wrong. They'd jump at it. Meanwhile I can continue, as long as I am still with you, to advise you about details which will save you money. . . . For example, when you've made the lake, you needn't plant English wild flowers round the water at once. You can take your time over it. You'll find all the arrangements very enjoyable. Then, in making the lake, you can leave out the island. That'll mean a big saving, and it's not really necessary, anyhow not at present. You'll have, of course, to make a copy of the Lake Pavilion. But you can't do that until I've built the original, so you see why it's so important for me to get on with it. It ought to be started immediately. All the plans are ready. One other point: it would pay you probably to sell the furniture and pictures in the house and to have exact copies made to furnish the new Renishaw. This is an age of copying and we ought to learn to make use of it. No one out there would know the difference, and it would mean a great saving.' . . . At this moment, those elegant cannibals, the jays, burst out from their dark castles in the trees, gave a screech and a mocking cackle of laughter, and my father, suddenly recalled to himself, said:

'I suppose it's time to start back now.'

# INDEX